MW01531540

GRUMPY OLD PARTY

GRUMPY OLD PARTY

20 Tips on How the Republicans Can Shed Their Anger,
Reclaim Their Respectability, *and* Win Back the White House

Constantinos E. Scaros

Foreword by John Catsimatidis Jr.
Chairman, New York College Republicans

WESTBOW
PRESS®
A DIVISION OF THOMAS NELSON
& ZONDERVAN

Copyright © 2015 Constantinos E. Scaros.

All rights reserved. No part of this book may be used or reproduced by any means, graphic, electronic, or mechanical, including photocopying, recording, taping or by any information storage retrieval system without the written permission of the author except in the case of brief quotations embodied in critical articles and reviews.

WestBow Press books may be ordered through booksellers or by contacting:

WestBow Press
A Division of Thomas Nelson & Zondervan
1663 Liberty Drive
Bloomington, IN 47403
www.westbowpress.com
1 (866) 928-1240

Because of the dynamic nature of the Internet, any web addresses or links contained in this book may have changed since publication and may no longer be valid. The views expressed in this work are solely those of the author and do not necessarily reflect the views of the publisher, and the publisher hereby disclaims any responsibility for them.

Any people depicted in stock imagery provided by Thinkstock are models, and such images are being used for illustrative purposes only. Certain stock imagery © Thinkstock.

Page 63 photograph provided by Dwight D. Eisenhower Presidential Library & Museum

ISBN: 978-1-5127-1325-1 (sc)
ISBN: 978-1-5127-1324-4 (hc)
ISBN: 978-1-5127-1323-7 (e)

Library of Congress Control Number: 2015916985

Print information available on the last page.

WestBow Press rev. date: 11/5/2015

To my wife, Anna, and my daughters, Ally and Melina.

Contents

Preface: Why I Wrote This Book

I enjoy writing books. They give me the opportunity to share my knowledge, express my thoughts, and hopefully sell a bunch of copies. At the moment, I can think of about a dozen books I'd like to write. But I chose to write this particular book now rather than later because I've seen Republicans make mistake after mistake over the past few years, and despite some recent presumable successes, I don't want to see them mess things up yet again.

I have voted in every presidential election since I was old enough to do so, and I've voted for Democrats, independents, and third-party candidates. But mostly, I have voted for Republicans. The last time I voted for a Republican for president, though, was in 2004. Not coincidentally, it was also the last time I was particularly enthusiastic about my choice. Essentially, when the Republicans are at their best, there is no one better; but when they're at their worst, they are not worth my vote. Why are the Republicans so hot and cold? Why do they swing like a wild pendulum from great to terrible election to election? I wrote this book to provide the answers because I for one would like a good reason to start voting for them again.

Perhaps most importantly, I should explain why I have the audacity to think I'm qualified to give the Republican Party advice on how to win presidential elections. I've spent decades studying, teaching, and writing about the American presidency. But even more notably, I have predicted every presidential election correctly since 1976, when I first started following them. Not the day before or the week before, but several months in advance. The only time I had to change my prediction was in 1992 because of Independent candidate Ross Perot's suspension and reactivation of his campaign—a surprise in both cases—which had a profound impact on the race.

Other than that aberration, I called every other election correctly as soon as both major party nominees were confirmed. Regarding the last four elections, the first time I heard the younger Bush, George W., speak, I knew he would win the election in 2000 (and again in 2004). I also knew from the moment the Republicans selected John McCain as their nominee in 2008 and Mitt Romney in 2012 that both would lose. It might seem peculiar to some why I had so much confidence in Bush and so little in the other two, considering both McCain and Romney were more-polished speakers than Bush and (especially in McCain's case) had more political experience when they won their GOP nominations. In this book, I explain why.

This is neither a scholarly treatise nor an exhaustive work of research. It's not particularly scientific or highly sophisticated. I envisioned it to be quick, readable, and rooted in common sense. I hope I have accomplished all three goals, and I hope this book reaches not only the GOP's powers-that-be and the nominees they field, but also the wider audience of the American people, whose power at the voting booth, when they choose to wield it, remains second to none.

Foreword

This book is a message to all my fellow Americans and particularly to my fellow millennials.

Before I graduated from New York University, I was President of its College Republican Club, and I am the current Chairman of the New York State College Republicans. If you have spent any time on a college campus lately or in a large city such as New York, you might at first blush think the phrase "Republican college student" or the title "College Republican Club President" sounds contradictory. People tend to think that politically motivated college students are a thing of the past. I disagree.

My experience in meeting and working with a wide array of politically motivated young people has given me uncommon insight into the current political climate and how our generation is reclaiming politics, how we are succeeding, how we are failing, and how we can do politics better than generations past did. I believe millennials today are a new kind of politically inclined. As a generation, we believe there are commonsense solutions to many of the political issues that plagued those in our parents' and grandparents' eras. Our challenge is to find ways to move past the partisan polarization and find the best solutions to these problems.

Being concerned about the problems themselves and having a willingness to participate politically to resolve them, however, are two different matters. One of the largest problems Americans—millennials in particular—face is a growing sense of political apathy caused by a flood of information. We live in a highly politicized media environment. The constant influx of information allows the casual news consumer only a limited knowledge of specific issues. This superficial acquisition is how we have ultimately come to gather information to make our voting decisions—not exactly a recipe for success by any conventional standard. Unfortunately, many Americans seem to shape their political views based on a single, predetermined news source that never wavers in its loyalty to a party or an ideology. If our Founding Fathers were so averse to listening to opinions that differed from their own, our country might be much different today, and not in a good way.

It is difficult to wade through all the opinions to actually learn about issues. The sheer volume of information shuts people off at the outset and makes young voters believe that becoming informed is an impossible game of catch-up. As political apathy rises, voter turnout among those age eighteen to twenty-nine remains abysmal. In the 2012 presidential election, only 40 percent in that age range voted. In the 2014 midterm elections, that number fell to 20 percent. There are many reasons people don't vote, and one I've often heard from political counterparts at school is the feeling that they have not found a candidate they could get behind, a candidate who represented them. As the political process turns off more people, the system enters a vicious cycle and creates even more political apathy. If that is the case, how about creating your own option?

When I mention that I am interested in politics, I usually get incredulous responses such as, "How can you put up with all the arguing?" The possibility for disagreement is what makes our democracy the best political system on the planet. As Americans, we have the right to free speech; we can voice our opinions about the government without fear of retribution. That right does not exist in so many other places in the world. We should never forget how powerful the agency of the American voter is. Sometimes, legislation takes time to discuss, negotiate, and pass, but thoughtful discourse and consideration are fundamental tenets of American democracy. Our society has some of the best-educated people in the world who use their knowledge and experience to collaborate on creating policies beneficial to all citizens.

I was a member of College Republicans for seven years (I began attending meetings in high school), and during that time, I noticed many people on both sides of the political aisle were already certain of their beliefs because of what they had learned before even stepping foot on campus. There is nothing wrong with being shaped by past experiences, but it always fascinates me to watch the development of students' beliefs over the course of a school year as they become exposed to ideas and experiences different from their own. Therefore, if you have found a politically inclined counterpart with whom to debate, you are already winning the battle.

I was recently given the opportunity to have dinner with a Republican presidential candidate. He said something that resonated with the room. "Democrats, Republicans, Liberals, and Conservatives … we all want the same thing: to make America great. The only difference is our opinions on how to get there." This is the trick: moving past the emotional arguments to speak and think logically and trust that the common interest in the prosperity, security, and general well-being of America is stronger than any difference that seeks to divide the populace.

It's easy to feel shut out of the political process due to being bombarded by the sheer volume of information and because some political campaigns utilize scare tactics; they spend millions to recruit voters by exploiting their fears. We need to stop allowing this rhetoric to turn us off and realize our government and its politics don't constitute a closed fortress that repels the common person. There has never been a born president. Every time we have elected a president, we have evaluated his merits, accomplishments, and abilities. It should be the highest goal of government to value and preserve the freedoms that make fair and free elections possible.

You are reading this book because for whatever reason, politics has piqued your interest. Good. That means you realize you have the ability to elect the people you think will best benefit our country. Why stop there? Why stop at trying to find the best candidate who most closely matches your opinions and beliefs? How about trying it out yourself? Run for a position on the school board, local office, or Congress. We need more people running for office who have specific ideas and who aren't afraid to say what they want to accomplish because they are scared of jeopardizing their potential to make politics a career. The best way to make politics more reachable to a generation of disinterested millennials is to have them talking about the issues that are most pressing for our future.

I am a Republican because I believe in the core value of personal freedom, and I view that party as the best feasible option for putting that into practice in a responsible manner to benefit our society. However, I write this plea for political participation to all millennials. Whether we are Republican, Democrat, or something in between, we need to start reenergizing the entire political spirit of our generation.

It is easier than ever to be involved in politics. We can become involved at literally the click of a button. We should be the most informed, active, and vocal generation yet.

But we are not.

I don't think our political system is hopeless. Every year, good candidates stand in front of voters who have become so apathetic that they don't care enough to bother to get to know them. These candidates have a messaging problem. They are simply not communicating well. They aren't finding ways to break through an entrenched media cycle.

Grumpy Old Party is most pointedly a message to the Republican Party about what it's doing wrong and how to fix that. More broadly, though, it is for anyone looking to connect and help others connect to millennials and all Americans. It will teach you how to look at things from multiple perspectives rooted in common sense. To formulate an opinion and stand by it confidently but remain open-minded enough to change your views. To reserve the right and embrace the privilege to be smarter tomorrow than you are today. And most of all, how to win elections and put those ideas into action.

—John Catsimatidis Jr.
Chairman, New York College Republicans
New York, July 2015

Acknowledgments

Many thanks to all the folks at WestBow Press for their careful attention in guiding this manuscript all the way through to publication.

To John Catsimatidis Jr. for writing a wonderful Foreword, and to David Collison, Gov. Michael Dukakis, Tricia Erickson, and Jimmy Kemp for their kind words of support about the book.

To Maryanne O'Neill for providing a fresh set of eyes in the final editing stages.

And, last but not least, to my family and friends for their continuous support.

Introduction: Where Did They Go Wrong?

Abraham Lincoln, widely considered the greatest president of all time and rarely ranked lower than second, was a Republican. His election cemented the rise of the Republican Party, whose main cause early on was the abolition of slavery.

Theodore Roosevelt, also consistently heralded as an elite member of the class of American presidents, was a Republican as well.

The largest electoral landslides in the nation's history (with the exception of the elections involving George Washington and James Monroe, who essentially ran unopposed), forty-nine states to one, were achieved by Republicans.[1]

In their century-and-a-half history, the Republicans elected more presidents than any other party. But they suffered a major and potentially

---

[1] In 1972 and 1984, respectively, Richard Nixon and Ronald Reagan won forty-nine out of fifty states. No candidate actually opposed George Washington in the two elections in which he ran for president, 1788 and 1792. Other nominees appear on record because at the time, the vice president was the person who received the second-highest number of votes. Essentially, the other candidates were running to become vice-president. By 1820, the Twelfth Amendment (ratified in 1804) provided for separate votes for president and vice president; President James Monroe was reelected unopposed.

lethal blow twice—when the 1929 stock market crash and ensuing Great Depression originated during Herbert Hoover's presidency, and when the Watergate scandal forced Richard Nixon to resign in 1974. But they were rescued from oblivion by two extremely popular presidents: Dwight D. Eisenhower in the 1950s and Ronald Reagan in the 1980s.

As a term of praise for having won the Civil War and having kept the nation together, the Republicans were dubbed the Grand Old Party, the GOP. After losing the popular vote in the 2000 presidential election, eking out a tough win in 2004, and losing in 2008 and particularly in 2012 to an incumbent on whose watch a listless economy couldn't push unemployment much below 8 percent, GOP might as well had stood for Grumpy Old Party. Republicans are angry and bitter, and they often grasp at straws to establish their identity. They are unaware of why all their presidential candidates in the post-Reagan era, except for George W. Bush, were destined to lose the moment they were nominated. Their brand of conservatism is a radical one that is out of touch with the vast majority of the American people—which is particularly telling considering the United States remains a center-right nation. Even if Reagan himself were to come back to life and run for president again, the Republicans would run him out of town, probably branding him an America-hating socialist.

The only question is whether Democrats in the near future will enjoy decades of unchallenged governance or if a third party will emerge and fill the void the GOP is fast creating despite its occasional electoral respites. Never mind the fiscal cliff we so often hear about; the Republicans are on the edge of a mental-health cliff, clinging to a flimsy twig, and scrambling to hold on to whatever semblance of sanity they have left.

Two other major parties in our nation's history have committed political suicide: the Federalists around 1800, and the Democrats around the 1860s. The former never recovered; the latter did, but only after several decades. The first and last Federalist president was John Adams. George Washington, who had Federalist ideas, never officially joined that party (or any political party for that matter). Despite being portrayed as a great Founder by some modern historians, Adams was notorious for implementing the Alien and Sedition Acts of 1798, which among other things put people in prison for daring to speak out against government policy. Imagine if that law were in effect today: "Don't like Barack Obama? Don't like John Boehner? Then it's off to jail with you!" Talk about big government run amok. Adams lost reelection to Thomas Jefferson, and the Federalists were never heard from again.

Fast forward to the 1850s and two listless Democratic presidents— Franklin Pierce and James Buchanan. They weren't bad people, just two men utterly incapable of dealing with the divisive issue of slavery and its inevitable consequence, the secession of the Southern states from the Union. That was only the beginning of the end. When Vice President Andrew Johnson, a Democrat, suddenly found himself president after Abraham Lincoln's assassination, he tried to block and reverse a considerable amount of the Republicans' reconstruction initiatives, which he considered too radical.[2] Some of Johnson's actions went too far in Congress' view, and so impeachment proceedings were brought against him. He was acquitted by just one vote. Politically, Johnson and the Democrats were done. Despite a couple of exceptions, the Democratic Party didn't fully recover until 1932, the year Franklin Delano Roosevelt was elected.

That brings us to the present day and why despite their seemingly resounding comeback in the November 2014 elections, the Republicans are poised to become the third major party in American history to self-destruct. They are delusional and disorganized. What makes the Republicans particularly pitiful is that their main rivals, the Democrats, are far from being in great shape themselves. Take away President Obama and the Clintons and the Democrats are as insignificant as they were in the days of George McGovern, Jimmy Carter, and Walter Mondale. That they are poised to emerge as the dominant party, then,

---

[2] Though Lincoln was a Republican, he had chosen Johnson as his running mate to create the appeal of a balanced ticket.

speaks volumes about the long-term bad shape the Republicans are in, by comparison.

Will the Republicans regain their glory, or will they, as did the Whig, Free Soil, and Bull Moose Parties, be reduced to a footnote that only history buffs would uncover?

Some think the Republican comeback in the 2014 midterm elections renders this advice obsolete, but quite the opposite is true. If anything, it makes it even more necessary, because even though the Republicans won, they have no clue as to why. They are like students who have to guess the correct answers on a multiple-choice test because they have no grasp of the material. In that case, whether they score correctly again the next time would hinge on a lucky guess. That's why, since 1994, when Republicans first regained control of Congress after forty years, they managed to lose their stronghold on Capitol Hill only a few years later rather than firmly establish themselves as America's dominant party—which they have the potential to become if only they would pay attention to what they must do.

Republican Party leaders, take note: this book is especially for you! The twenty tips herein are for your benefit so you can shed your anger, reclaim your respectability, and win back the White House. Pay attention—the lesson is about to begin.

Part I: Foundations

The first five tips are part of the category of "Foundations." They aren't issue specific. Rather, they are what the Republican Party must become not only to be competitive with the Democrats but also to become once again superior to them.

Tip 1: It's Likability, Stupid!

Even before Election Night 2012 was over, once it became apparent that Barack Obama was going to fend off Mitt Romney's challenge and win a second presidential term, Republican leaders and their sympathizers began offering explanations about what went wrong, proving yet again they had absolutely no clue. The political catchphrase "It's the economy, stupid!" became popular during the 1992 election, when it appeared that incumbent President George H. W. Bush wouldn't be reelected because he seemed out of touch with how the economy negatively impacted quality of life for millions of average Americans. Many thought that it would be all about the economy in 2012 as well. They were wrong. "It's likability, stupid!"

We can pick apart the multiple theories about why Romney lost the election, but it really boils down to one: people just didn't like him. Granted, once they realized Romney was their only chance to beat Obama, Republicans made do with what they had. They were like the guy who wanted his new car in hunter-green but found out he had to wait three months for it and talked himself into thinking he really wanted the midnight-blue one in the showroom all along.

Answer this, Republicans: suppose neither Barack Obama nor any other Democrat had been in the running in 2012 and that the next president of the United States would be whoever won the GOP Primary. In that case, how many of you really would have rooted for Romney to win? If Obama or any other Democrat hadn't been in the equation, if it had been simply a direct vote among eight or nine GOP candidates, the winner becoming president, would your first choice really have been Mitt Romney? Too many Republicans were gun-shy about backing their true favorite—whomever he or she might have been—because they thought Romney was the safest choice to defeat Obama. (More on that later, in Tip 4: Stop Playing It Safe! Define Your Ideals and the Votes Will Take Care of Themselves.)

Think about likability another way: when was the last time a candidate clearly less liked than his opponent won the White House? Let's define *like* not in terms of partisan or ideological compatibility but on personality. Let's go back to the modern-day Republican revolution that began on November 4, 1980, when Ronald Reagan won in a landslide. Did the voters really like his opponent, Jimmy Carter, or his 1984 rival, Walter Mondale, better than they liked the charismatic and affable Gipper? In 1988, did voters unequivocally like the technocratic Michael Dukakis better than the man who beat him, George H. W. Bush? Even Bill Clinton's opponents concede that they've never seen anyone electrify a room like he did. Did the voters, then, really like Bush Sr. and Bob Dole better than Clinton in 1992 and 1996 respectively?

Bush's son, George W., endured a complicated presidency. In terms of likability, however, he was famously referred to as "a guy you'd want to have a beer with." Did the voters really like better the sighing, droning Al Gore, whom Bush defeated in 2000, or the caustic, acerbic John Kerry, who lost to Bush four years later? In his first presidential campaign (2008), Barack Obama was described as a rock star. Was the ornery septuagenarian John McCain really the more likable of the two?

That brings us to Romney, and we all would be hard pressed to find someone less likable, less even than an incumbent president (Obama) under whose first term the economy grew at a snail's pace and joblessness

had not waned. Repeatedly, the candidate with the better personality—
the one who is liked more—wins the election.

Despite a first term in which the economy never fully rebounded,
in which an additional $4 trillion was added to the massive national
debt, a stimulus package that failed to bring down unemployment,
and sweeping health care reform was pushed through amid bitter
partisan contention and utter confusion, Obama never stopped being
likable. Sure, not by the millions of Obama-bashers who'd do just about
anything to make sure he wouldn't be reelected, but by his supporters.
Even when they admitted he wasn't doing a particularly good job,
they still liked him. Quite notably, Obama's likability numbers fell by
June 2014, a few months ahead of the November midterm elections.
Not surprisingly, many Democratic congressional candidates distanced
themselves from him. Take note: likability matters.

Anyone who owned a television in America during the 1970s
remembers the era's top-rated sitcom, *All in the Family*. That show broke
new boundaries in television comedy by daring to establish as its main
character Archie Bunker, a loudmouth, blue-collar conservative who
minced no words when it came to attacking blacks, Hispanics, Jews,
homosexuals, feminists, and any other group he felt was an obstacle
between himself—a WASP—and his share of the American dream. But
the show's creator, Norman Lear, knew that to sell Archie successfully to
the American public, Archie would have to be likable. Carroll O'Connor
played the role brilliantly, and it was particularly impressive that
O'Connor was precisely the type of bleeding-heart liberal against which
Archie always railed.[3] Though millions of Americans disagreed with
Archie ideologically, they laughed at his jokes and applauded instances
when his positive qualities shone through: displays of tenderness to his
family when it really counted, refusal to have an extramarital affair, and
many others. *All in the Family* was the top-rated show in the country

---

[3] Many Archie Bunker fans were shocked to learn that Carroll O'Connor, the actor
who portrayed him so brilliantly, was actually far to the left of Archie, and they
were shocked when O'Connor appeared in a 1980 commercial endorsing liberal
Independent presidential candidate John Anderson.

because even though its main character spewed lines considered so offensive that they had never been attempted on television prior to that, he was nonetheless likable.

Republicans, you can waste your time listening to your high-priced consultants and their self-serving polls and charts, and you can throw bad money after good in a losing effort, but it's time you realize that if you want to win back the White House, it all boils down to three words: "It's likability, stupid!"

Tip 2: Lose the Angry Tone

To be simultaneously angry and likable is theoretically possible but difficult. Closely related to Tip 1: It's Likability, Stupid! and crucial to correct if the GOP expects to win is the necessity that Republicans lose their angry tone. Think back to the most successful Republican by far over the past fifty years—Ronald Reagan. Do you ever remember him being angry? As he would prepare to speak, his face would light up as he slightly lowered and tilted his head, smiled, and delivered the punch line. Consider, for example, his characterization of the economy and his opponent, in 1980: "A recession is when your neighbor loses his job, a depression is when you lose *your* job, and recovery is when *Jimmy Carter* loses *his* job." There were no outbursts of "He's ruining this country!" or "He's the worst president ever!"

Talk radio is dominated by conservatives. Angry conservatives. Rush Limbaugh, who is more sarcastic than angry, is the tip of the iceberg. Think about Sean Hannity, Mark Levin, Laura Ingraham, Michael Savage, and scores of others. An interesting experiment would be to ask someone who understands little or no English to listen to any of those radio personalities for about fifteen minutes. Without even understanding what they said, the person would be able to discern how they say it: angrily. What Republicans haven't realized—not just those on radio and TV but also those in office—is that sometimes the right tone will sway more voters than the right answer.

Consider this example as an illustration. Clerk works at a store owned by two bosses, Democrat and Republican. Merchant is about to deliver goods to the store, and Clerk must pay Merchant $1,000 for the goods minus $385 the Merchant owes the store. Clerk receives the goods and pays Merchant $715. Clerk tells his two bosses about the transaction, and Democrat, not having figured out that Clerk should have paid Merchant $615 instead of $715, says, "Good job, Clerk!" But Republican, who immediately figures out the mistake in his head, lashes out at the two of them. To Clerk: "You're an idiot! How could you pay an extra $100? Don't you know that 1,000 minus 385 is 615, not 715? Are you *that* stupid? You're either a complete moron or you have some secret side deal worked out with Merchant and so you're stealing from us! Get out of my sight!"

He says to Democrat: "And you are an even *bigger* idiot! At least Clerk is some dope with no future, but you—you're my business partner, and you can't even do simple arithmetic! What a jerk you are. I can't believe we're in business together. I'm embarrassed to call you my partner!"

Democrat turns to Clerk and chuckles. "I guess we both goofed."

Suppose the argument causes a rift between Democrat and Republican, and they sell the business, and each opens a new store. Democrat and Republican (despite the latter's earlier tirade) make the same offer to Clerk: "Come work in my new store." Republicans, can you guess which of the two bosses Clerk will choose?

Give up? Here's the answer—Clerk goes home to mull over the offers and thinks aloud, "If I work for Democrat, we're both careless with numbers, and we may slowly bankrupt the business in a year or two. That's not a good thing. But it will be a good year or two because he'll be nice to me. However, if I work for Republican, he's got a much better business sense. The store probably will be a big success, and I may even get a raise and a promotion. But I'd be subjected to being yelled at, berated, and embarrassed probably every single day. No amount of money is worth that. I'll work for Democrat."

Before we delve into the moral of this story, let's keep the following things in mind: none of this is to suggest that Republicans are categorically nasty, that Democrats are categorically inept, or that Republicans necessarily have a better business sense or mathematical aptitude than do Democrats. The example illustrates, however, that like Clerk, voters may often vote against their practical interests because they like another candidate's tone better.

Think about leaders in all walks of life and the folks who follow them. People follow those who are smart, confident, funny, kind, compassionate, inspiring, imaginative, and charming, among other attractive qualities. When was the last time you heard anyone say, "Hey! I want to follow that guy. He's angry!"

Never mind the midterm successes of 2014. The Republicans didn't win that election as much as the Democrats lost it. In fact, the GOP may be in even greater danger of losing in 2016 because they have yet to shed their anger.

Lesson to be learned, Republicans: uber-aggressiveness is unattractive. Lose the angry tone!

Tip 3: Credibility Trumps Quantity

The credibility of a campaign against a presidential rival is more important than the quantity of zingers hurled. The GOP in 2012 could have taken the high road with principled, well-placed criticism against Barack Obama on a few topics, particularly those discussed in Tip 1: It's Likability, Stupid! namely, the weak economy, high unemployment, and disorganized health care reform. Thinking instead that quantity was more important than credibility, the Republicans and their minions threw the kitchen sink at the incumbent president; many of the accusations were completely unfounded and utterly absurd.

The name of Tip 3: Credibility Trumps Quantity, is rather purposefully selected, specifically the word *trumps*, to conjure images of a man who on occasion has been the epitome of what not to say: Donald Trump. In Trump's defense, he has made a lot of astute, even profound statements about an array of domestic and foreign affairs issues over the years. He entered the 2016 presidential race as a Republican and made a big impact; at the time of publication – Fall 2015 – he was the party frontrunner in all major polls. But Trump almost completely destroyed his credibility some time back when he joined the small but squeaky bandwagon of the birthers, who purported the utterly ridiculous theory that President Obama hadn't been born in the United States. That contention doesn't merit the legitimate debate other issues do: such as, whether trickle-down economics works or whether diplomacy, sanctions, or military force would be more effective in dealing with Iran. The birther issue deserves to be taken to task for its utter lack of logic.

The argument was that the birth certificate that confirms Barack Obama was born on August 4, 1961 in Honolulu, Hawaii is a fake. The implication was that Obama hadn't been born in the United States and was thereby ineligible to be president of the United States because he wasn't a natural-born citizen, as the US Constitution requires presidents to be.

Before we explore why that argument was devoid of common sense, let's look at the possible consequences if in fact it were true. Obama would be removed from office, and Vice President Joe Biden would become president. Beyond a rather simple transfer of power, however, it would create the biggest scandal that ever rocked the nation—one that would cause unspeakable embarrassment and shake the very foundation on which our country was built. The stock market would be in a free fall not experienced since the great crash in 1929, and the economy would plummet perhaps to record-low depths.

On August 9, 1974, Richard Nixon resigned the presidency of the United States because it appeared almost inevitable that he would have been impeached for an attempt to cover up the Watergate incident. Very likely, he would have been convicted and not only removed from office but also subjected to a criminal trial. Nixon's successor, Gerald Ford, sensed that a prolonged trial of a former president, one that might result in the shocking image of Nixon being dragged off in handcuffs like a common hoodlum, would be incredibly damaging to the nation's psyche. Ford decided to pardon Nixon instead.

In doing so, Ford essentially sealed his own political doom. It is widely believed that the Nixon pardon is why Ford lost the election in 1976 to Jimmy Carter, but years later, he was vindicated for having put the nation's well-being ahead of his personal aspirations.

Why then would the birthers even want to risk unraveling what undoubtedly would become a national tragedy at least as destructive as Watergate if not more so if it were true? Is their blind anti-Obama obsession so strong that they would we willing to sink our nation or cripple it indefinitely just to get one guy out of office? That said, let's now turn to why the birther argument makes no sense.

First, two Honolulu newspapers had published announcements of Obama's birth in Hawaii a few days after he was born.[4] If the announcements were phony, it would have meant that whoever conspired to fabricate Obama's American birth did so not merely a few years before 2008 in hopes of molding him into a legitimate presidential candidate but all the way back in 1961, when he was only a couple of days old! Yes, way back in 1961, when Obama was a baby that no one could have predicted might have been smart, healthy, a good speaker, and telegenic—qualities essential to electability. And why did they name this secret spy "Barack Hussein Obama" rather than something more innocuous for mainstream America such as "Brandon Howard Olson?" That would be like conspiring to transform a baby boy born today into a powerful gangster in America forty years from now who would pose as a legitimate businessman and naming him "Al Capone."

Next, such a conspiracy started back in 1961 would have had to have extended beyond fooling the newspaper staffers in charge of the Notices-Births section in 1961 because Obama had to clear numerous hurdles before being elected president. He went through the admissions process at Columbia and Harvard Universities, a review by the Illinois Bar, background checks by the Illinois and US Senates, and then of course one of the most well-organized political tandems in modern history able to dig up anything worth digging up: the Clintons. Were all those verification systems so inept that those monitoring them could have been duped so easily like a bouncer at a club fooled by a minor's fake ID? Really?

Perhaps most significantly, even if Obama had been born out of the country, he still would have been qualified to be president of the

---

[4] The two newspapers were the *Honolulu Advertiser* and the *Honolulu Star-Bulletin*.

United States; the conditions under which a person may be deemed a natural-born citizen are in Section 1401 of the US Code. As one might imagine, being physically born on US soil is one way. But there are others. Subsection (g) clearly states that a natural-born citizen is also

> a person born outside the geographical limits of the United States and its outlying possessions of parents one of whom is an alien, and the other a citizen of the United States who, prior to the birth of such person, was physically present in the United States or its outlying possessions for a period or periods totaling not less than five years, at least two of which were after attaining the age of fourteen years.

That brings us to President Obama's parents: his father, Barack Obama Sr., had been born in Kenya, which made him an alien. Obama's mother, Ann Dunham, had been born in Kansas. She traveled throughout the United States during her early years, and it wasn't until 1967, just shy of her twenty-fifth birthday, that she settled in Indonesia. Clearly, she had been present in the United States for more than five years (twenty-four years), including a great deal more than two after she had reached age fourteen (ten years).

For all those reasons, the birther argument is incorrect. Its existence can be chalked up to any of three possibilities or combinations thereof, none of which would be appealing to the electorate: 1) drawing a careless conclusion without having examined the situation carefully; 2) being incapable of applying the basic rules of logic and common sense to draw a conclusion; and 3) lying or having reckless disregard for the truth in the name of discrediting a political opponent.

The birther argument tops the list of criticism against Obama that severely damages the birthers' credibility, and that is why it's not enough for some Republicans simply to ignore birthers when they utter such absurdities. They must go further; they must express outrage. The

GOP should unequivocally and emphatically condemn any unfounded, illogical accusations against a sitting president as an official part of its platform. As for Donald Trump, he soared in the polls when he entered the 2016 race and not-so-coincidentally, didn't bring up the birth certificate nonsense.

A distant second but nonetheless ridiculous accusation hurled at President Obama is that he is really a Muslim in disguise. Regarding that issue, the Republicans should say, "First of all, he's not a Muslim, and second, even if he were, so what?" Failure by the GOP to do that practically screams their intentions: "Hey, we may not believe it ourselves, but if saying he's a Muslim frightens racists and xenophobes and gets us their vote, we'll take it!" Fine, Republicans, go with that approach because in every twenty Americans, there's one Islamophobe who buys into the baseless propaganda and votes against Obama, and nineteen who will find the statement offensive to their sense of intelligence and decency. And pay attention to this part; it's *really* important: among those nineteen are some who would have voted Republican but voted for Obama simply to spite the Muslim-theory demagogues.

What makes this secret Muslim contention even more absurd is that the same people accused Obama of harboring the anti-American rhetoric espoused by Jeremiah Wright, the reverend at the Trinity Christian Church Obama attended regularly for twenty years. Let's get this straight: Obama attended a Christian church for most of his adult life, smoked cigarettes for even longer than that, drinks beer (even says that he microbrews some in the White House), eats hot dogs, and has killed more Muslims (via drone strikes) than any modern president—and yet supposedly he's a Muslim. If Obama is a Muslim, he sure is bad at it!

Back to Obama's purported anti-Americanism, a tenuous hypothesis largely centered on his connection to Reverend Wright and his loose association with former domestic terrorist Bill Ayers. First, let us play out the argument to its logical (if there is one) conclusion: a man who hates the United States has battled incredibly hard to become its leader—a job that arguably is one of the most stressful and most dangerous in the world, whose conditions extend to the officeholder's family. Why then would Obama risk the health, life, and limb of his wife and two daughters as well as himself to be in charge of a nation he so despises? "In order to destroy it from within," the conspiracy theorists might respond. Apparently, they've never heard of checks and balances, a cornerstone of our system of government. The president is not the king—the Founding Fathers specifically designed it that way. Without even addressing how Obama feels about the United States, let's put it this way: Obama (or any other president) couldn't destroy America even if he tried.

The Founders, of course, designed the American presidency to be limited in power for a specific purpose. Having declared their independence from a powerful dictator, King George III of England, the last thing they wanted was another guy in power telling them what to do. Though Americans sometimes think and fear the president can do anything, the reality is that a president's powers go only so far precisely so a president cannot become an unstoppable dictator.

Obama, a constitutional law professor, certainly would have known that ahead of time, wouldn't he? It's not as if he became president and then said, "Wait a minute. You mean I don't have the power to destroy America?" Even in the unlikely instance that he actually thought he could have done damage to the United States only to be disappointed in learning about our three-branch system of government, why would he have run for a second term? Wouldn't he simply have thought, *Bad idea. This destroying America from within thing. Won't work*, and simply stepped aside and called it a day?

"Alright," the naysayers might respond, "maybe he doesn't hate America, but he certainly wants to turn it into a socialist European nation!" Socialist? By leading the way in his first term to cutting the payroll tax and not raising anyone's income tax by a single penny?[5] By

---

[5] Eventually, the top tax rates under Obama returned to the Clinton levels of the 1990s, but those were still lower than the levels established by Ronald Reagan's sweeping tax cuts a decade earlier.

allowing the Federal Reserve to operate autonomously and choosing the New York Fed's president, Timothy Geithner, as his first secretary of the treasury? Or by his mandate that every American must purchase health insurance, which was originally a Republican idea rooted in the no-free-ride notion that the insured shouldn't have to foot the bill for the uninsured?

Once again, Republicans, here is how you can reclaim your credibility: question Obama's philosophy that the government is the best resource to restore economic growth. Point out his failures to bring spending under control and to reduce unemployment. Emphasize that he leads from behind too much, particularly on the world stage. But don't call him a foreign-born, America-hating, socialist Muslim, because when you do, you make complete fools of yourselves.

And if some rogue talk-show host or blogger makes those comments on your behalf, denounce the comments and the commentator alike. You don't need to say a hundred negative things about Obama and whomever his Democratic successor might be, because if even just ten of the accusations are off the wall, you'll neutralize the impact your other ninety negative things might have otherwise had.

Try the opposite tack instead; criticize Obama about ten things, or five, or even just three. Stick to those few criticisms as long as they're valid and important. Remember—credibility trumps quantity.

Tip 4: Stop Playing It Safe! Define Your Ideals and the Votes Will Take Care of Themselves

In many ways, Tip 1: It's Likability, Stupid! is the most important point of this book because without likability, a presidential candidate is bound to lose. But the reason Reagan and George W. won whereas Dole, McCain, and Romney lost had to do with more than their likability. The other common thread was that the winners didn't play it safe. Reagan's famous speech in 1975 called upon the Republicans to raise "a banner of no pale pastels, but bold colors which make it unmistakably clear where we stand." The GOP responded by nominating Reagan himself in 1980. He won. Twice.

In 1988, they shifted gears and handed the nomination to George H. W. Bush, who was Reagan's vice president but not necessarily his ideological heir. Bush won anyway but only because Reagan had been so incredibly popular that Bush rode his coattails to victory and because Bush's opponent, Michael Dukakis, ran an admirably noble but largely ineffective campaign.

The next time around, Bush lost. In 1996, the Republicans again went with the safe choice, nominating their longstanding Senate leader

Bob Dole, who was predictably defeated by incumbent Bill Clinton by a comfortable margin. Dole ran a respectable campaign but never had a chance.

Bush's son, George W., won in 2000 and 2004, and he, more so than his dad, seemed like a successor to Reagan in terms of passion and ideology. But in 2008, the Republicans played the safe card again; they turned to another longtime bridesmaid, John McCain, who not surprisingly lost. Not having learned their lesson, they fielded the innocuous Mitt Romney in 2012, losing yet again.

Newsflash: the 270 Strategy—aiming for the meager goal of amassing 270 electoral votes, the thinnest of majorities—is a bad one. And Karl Rove is not going to be correct every time. In American professional football, the two conference winners face off against one another in the Super Bowl. The teams have two weeks to prepare; does either devise a strategy to win the game just by one point? That would be a ludicrous game plan; it wouldn't decide that the champion was clearly the better team. Similarly, the 270 Strategy does nothing more than expose the party in question as shallow charlatans whose only goal is to obtain and maintain power; it leaves the nation as divided after Election Day as it was before.

Instead, Republicans need to establish who they are and what they believe in and publicize those ideals. If their message is good, votes will take care of themselves. If the message is bad, they don't deserve to win in the first place.

Things were much easier for the GOP during the Reagan years and not only because the Party's standard bearer was dubbed the Great Communicator. In those days, the Democrats were a true tax-and-spend party. It seemed their answer to everything was a government program. Those Democrats of yesteryear made fitting targets for many of Reagan's one-liners such as,

- "The nearest thing to eternal life we will ever see on this earth is a government program."

- "The government is like a baby's alimentary canal, with a happy appetite at one end and no responsibility at the other."
- "The most terrifying words in the English language are 'I'm from the government and I'm here to help.'"
- "Government is not the solution to the problem, government *is* the problem."

However, when George H. W. Bush tried his version of those same lines in 1992, they failed. Republicans mistakenly blamed Bush's defeat on independent candidate Ross Perot, who earned 19 percent of the vote nationwide. What they failed to realize, though, is that Perot probably took more votes away from Bush's main challenger, Clinton, than from the president. If anyone should have been nervous, it should have been Clinton, because Perot's presence in the race effectively cut into Clinton's near-unanimous share of the anti-Bush vote.

The biggest impact Perot had on the vote was not that Bush lost (most likely he would have lost anyway) but that Clinton won by less than a majority (he received only 43 percent of the vote). Others said Bush couldn't deliver Reagan's message because he wasn't nearly as good a speaker. That part is true; in terms of inspiring the masses, Bush wasn't in Reagan's league. Why then had that same Bush won on that message four years earlier?

In 1988, Bush overwhelmed Democrat Michael Dukakis in a 426–111 electoral landslide (one Dukakis elector cast a symbolic vote for Dukakis's running mate, Lloyd Bentsen, as a protest of the Electoral College). The difference? Bill Clinton characterized himself as a different kind of Democrat than Dukakis, Mondale, Carter, McGovern, and others. In fact, Clinton exposed Bush's message in 1992's first general election debate as outmoded and outdated by pointing out Bush was "trying to run against Lyndon Johnson and Jimmy Carter and everybody in the world but me in this race."[6]

---

[6] Clinton Bush Perot Debate 1, October 11, 1992.

Actually, many Republicans have figured that out. As the saying goes, this is not your father's Democratic Party. Many even realize that despite all the hoopla to the contrary, Barack Obama is that type of centrist Democrat too! (Yes, Republicans, he is a centrist, not a leftist—and the sooner you learn that, the better off politically you'll be.) Besides, Republicans realize that the voters are all too aware of the Republicans' runaway spending, particularly in between election years 2000 and 2006, when they dominated Congress. So how could they possibly claim with a straight face to be the party of fiscal responsibility? Their answer? Label Obama a dangerous, foreign-born Muslim and double down on social issues. The result? They almost completely alienated voters of color, decreased their support among women, and—despite what may be only a brief reprieve in 2014—are effectively on the road to becoming a fringe party of a diminishing group of angry white males.

The GOP's selection of Mitt Romney as its 2012 presidential nominee epitomizes the 270 Strategy. I spent a good deal of time in Tip 1: It's Likability, Stupid! explaining why Romney was not a suitable candidate, so there is no need to repeat those points. It's important to restate, however, that the most appealing thing about Romney to Republican voters was his potential to beat Obama. The strategy was to remove the solid blue and solid red states from the equation and concentrate on a handful of swing states. Romney, they thought, would have won those. Their monumental miscalculation, about which they had no clue, of course, was twofold: they underestimated the number of voters who would stick with Obama even though the president's first term had been far from perfect, and they overestimated how many voters would embrace Romney.

It's time, Republicans, to identify who you really are regardless of the outcome. Are you really a party that under no conditions would agree to increase any taxes? Do you really stand for outlawing abortion and same-sex marriage? Do you believe climate change is grossly overdramatized and barely makes the list of the top 500 national concerns? Do you want Americans to retain the freedom to decide whether or not to purchase health care instead of having the government require them to do so? Do you think there should be absolutely no limits on individual gun ownership rights? Or are you adopting those points of view in an attempt to magnify your differences with the Democrats?

What are your priorities? Social issues? Economic issues? National security issues? Figure out who you are, clearly define your positions, and stick to them year in, year out. To the extent that the Democrats are different from you, emphasize those differences. If the Democrats have the same or almost the same viewpoint on a particular issue as you do, acknowledge it. Say, "We're right, and the Democrats are right too." Stop inventing false differences with the Democrats where there aren't any just so you can play the role of agent of change. And, above all, stop playing it safe. Define your ideals, and the votes will take care of themselves.

Tip 5: Stop Dumbing Down the Republican Party

Before adopting the principle of not dumbing down the Republican Party, let's be clear that *dumb* in this discussion doesn't mean lack of natural intelligence but lack of qualifications to hold political office and at times an utter disregard for them. It means that when John McCain plucked Sarah Palin from the obscurity of the Alaska governorship and propelled her into the national spotlight to be his running mate, which positioned her potentially a heartbeat away from the presidency, she was not unintelligent. Rising from modest means and without political connections to become the governor of a state—even one as sparsely populated as Alaska—takes a good amount of ability and smarts without question. And to do that job and raise five children at the same time is commendable and remarkable. But Sarah Palin at that time lacked enough understanding of domestic and especially foreign issues. Therefore, while Palin herself wasn't dumb, McCain's having picked her as his running mate and the thunderous support she received from millions was a prime example of the dumbing down of the Republican Party.

Sarah Palin loves Alaska. She seems to know every square inch of her state. She eats, sleeps, and breathes Alaska. She would make a great president of Alaska, even queen of Alaska. She's not dumb; it's just that in 2008, her brain's hard drive was filled disproportionately with information about Alaska and not enough about the other forty-nine states and the rest of the world.[7] For those reasons, it's not enough to say, "We need a conservative woman on the ticket, one with spunk and charisma. Hey! There's one. Let's make her the VP nominee!" That's a good example of dumbing down the party.

Samuel Joseph Wurzelbacher, better known as Joe the Plumber, was also plucked from obscurity in 2008 when he asked Candidate Obama a question during a campaign rally, to which Obama uttered a response that included the words "spread the wealth." His remark, as they say in social media circles, went viral.

In yet another example of how Republicans didn't follow Tip 3: Credibility Trumps Quantity, they paraded Joe around as if he were the poster boy for capitalism, the underdog protagonist fighting the good fight against the scourge of socialism about to be spread throughout the land by the dreaded Obama Machine.

But Joe's story fits better here in Tip 5: Stop Dumbing Down the Republican Party, because in 2012, Joe ran for Congress. Joe figured he was an ordinary guy with a high school diploma and no political experience—heck, why not run for national office? As with Palin, there is nothing to indicate that Joe lacks natural intelligence, nor is there anything less noble about being a plumber than a brain surgeon. But today, candidates for public office—for any job, in fact—should take their personal experience and qualifications more seriously. "But the Founding Fathers wanted average Americans to run for public office— they didn't want career politicians," some will retort. True, but in those days, the average American had an entirely different and markedly superior grasp of domestic and international affairs than did the typical twenty-first-century American.

---

[7] Since 2008, because of her vice presidential nomination and ensuing public life as a political commentator, Sarah Palin has learned a great deal more about the United States and the world.

John Quincy Adams, for example, hardly considered one of our greatest presidents, rose every morning as a child to study an array of subjects intensely—not just homework but also religion, philosophy, and other subjects that shaped his journey of lifelong learning. Yes, lifelong learning. Intellectual curiosity. Learning for the sake of learning, not as some admission ticket to landing a job. No offense to Joe, but all other things being equal, a plumber in the 1700s was probably far more well rounded and would have made a more formidable candidate for public office.

"Well, then, what about Reagan?" some might ask. "He was an actor who was only an average student at a little-known college, and yet he became a great president." Yes, all that's true. But Reagan had been governor of California—the most populous state in the nation—for eight years, and he spent several decades crafting his vision of how to lead America before he decided to run for president. It's not as if he decided to take a lunch break while filming *Bedtime for Bonzo* one day and thought, *Gee, you know what? I think I'll run for president!*

"Okay, that was Reagan," the naysayer might continue. "But what about Obama? He was just a community organizer." Granted, Obama didn't have a particularly impressive resume prior to seeking the nation's highest office, and he had been a community organizer. But he was also a constitutional law professor, an attorney, a US Senator for four years, and an Illinois State Senator eight years before that. Face it, Republicans; you struck out with the likes of Palin and Wurzelbacher. Take your lumps, cut your losses, and try again.

In 2008, Obama said, "We should be emphasizing foreign languages in our schools from an early age." Well, that's all the dumbing-down and Manchurian candidate crowd needed to hear to turn Obama's statements into a mission to wipe out English in America and eradicate any Western European influence on American culture.

Another rarely mentioned president, James A. Garfield, would verbally answer questions in Greek while writing the answers in Latin at the same time. The physician and author Martin H. Fischer famously said, "Any man who does not make himself proficient in at least two languages other than his own is a fool." But there went the Republicans, ridiculing Obama for inspiring our nation's children to broaden their intellectual horizons.

Formal education is certainly not the answer to everything, but let's compare two of the most well-known commentators on the right—Rush Limbaugh and Sean Hannity, with their counterparts on the left, Bill Maher and Rachel Maddow. Maher and Maddow graduated from Ivy League universities (Cornell and Harvard respectively), and Maddow earned a PhD from Oxford. Limbaugh and Hannity are college dropouts. That doesn't make Maher and Maddow smarter, but why is it that nowadays the Republicans seem to glorify *under*education?

Intellectual conservatism didn't die with William F. Buckley Jr. There are plenty of brilliant and sophisticated conservatives around—Peggy Noonan, Thomas Sowell, Cal Thomas, and George Will are among the more prominent—who have been trampled upon by the red-meat, rightwing bloodhounds. Why read a complex treatise when a three-hour radio show that's one big attack ad requires less brainpower? We Americans probably would be in better physical shape collectively if the remote control hadn't been invented, but are any of us willing to give up that precious device and rise from our seat every time we want to change the channel or adjust the volume? Similarly, we Americans are fine with using our brains when we have to, but when Limbaugh and Hannity spoon-feed ready-made thoughts to us, we aren't going to spit them out and say, "No! Please make my brain work harder than that."

Another example of the false sense of security Republicans have gained since the 2014 midterm elections is that they actually think they have reversed the dumb-down strategy. All the proof needed to refute that claim is the backlash against First Lady Michelle Obama in her quest to combat child obesity. Yes, child obesity. The first lady dared to strive for healthier kids in America, but because she was married to the Republicans' public enemy number one, by default, they felt they had to ridicule and condemn everything she said. Congratulations, Republicans; you've cornered the market on defending obesity.

The party of Lincoln, Theodore Roosevelt, Eisenhower, and Reagan, the ideology espoused by intellectual giants such as Milton Friedman and James Q. Wilson, deserves better. Stop dumbing down the Republican Party.

Top: Abraham Lincoln
Bottom: Theodore Roosevelt

Abraham Lincoln is considered by many to be the greatest president ever. Theodore Roosevelt is also very highly ranked and was immensely popular. Both were Republicans. What happened? When did the Grand Old Party become the Grumpy Old Party?

Top: George Washington
Bottom: John Quincy Adams

In his Farewell Address to the nation, George Washington warned against forming political parties. He knew the nastiness that comes with the territory.

John Quincy Adams, even as his reelection bid was unraveling before his eyes, refused to campaign because he considered it undignified. Nowadays, the opposite behavior—win at any cost—is the norm.

Top: Benjamin Franklin
Bottom: James A. Garfield

Founding Father Benjamin Franklin was so smart that people thought he was capable of doing anything.

Republican James A. Garfield could verbally answer a question in Greek while simultaneously writing the answer in Latin. Can someone please tell today's Republicans that being smart and well educated are *good* things?

Top: An oil well in the United States
Bottom: US antiaircraft missiles

The two best ways to keep American safe is to "Drill, baby, drill" for as much oil as possible, which will render rogue nations and terrorist groups utterly irrelevant, and to have an impenetrable missile defense shield that would make nuclear weapons seem as harmless as marshmallows.

Part II: Basic Dos and Don'ts

The next four tips begin with not falling into the trap of trying to be like Democrats. The rest of the book will explain how regarding specific issues, the Republicans must be different from what they are now but also different from the Democrats.

Tip 6: Don't Try to Be Democrats

On first impression, the very thought of Republicans—especially today's doggedly stubborn, relentlessly uncompromising Republicans—trying to be like Democrats is unimaginable. It's not as if Republicans would suddenly start to raise taxes, increase spending, or support same-sex marriage, but they would try—and have tried—appealing to groups of voters who traditionally vote Democratic, namely, people of color and immigrants.

Reaching out to those groups is a great idea, of course, from the noble perspective of being a party that makes everyone feel included and welcome and from a practical perspective of maximizing the opportunity to gain more votes. The problem then is not that Republicans reach out to these groups but the way by which they do. Tip 7: Don't "Latinofy" the Message Artificially, Tip 12: Reclaiming Race Relations, and Tip 16: Winning on Immigration provide specific observations on what the Republicans are doing wrong and instructions on how they can do things right.

The remainder of the tips in this book are devoted to reclaiming Republican strongholds that have been ceded to the Democrats in recent years as well as winning on other issues that also until recently had been up for grabs. Republicans seem to have a problem controlling the thermostat; they make it too hot or too cold. They blame their losses on candidates who are too quick to compromise, but they often seem to gravitate to the safest choice, the one who in the primaries might appear to be the most "Democratic" among Republicans.

Each of the five major parties in American history—which in chronological order of establishment are the Federalists, the Democratic-Republicans, the Democrats, the Whigs, and the Republicans—was founded based on a single, overriding principle. The Federalists wanted to maintain a strong central government, whereas the Democratic-Republicans were more in favor of states' rights and individual liberties. The Democrats spoke for the ordinary Americans who had been seemingly cast aside by the rich and powerful, and the Whigs wanted to tilt the balance of power to Congress so the president wouldn't wield the omnipotence of a king.

The Republican Party was founded on a reason more noble than that of most if not all the other parties, the abolition of slavery. One of the reasons the United States is the greatest superpower in the history of the world—greatest not only in military might but in human decency—is because its citizens (soldiers in the North) risked and lost their own lives to establish someone else's (the slaves in the South) independence. Granted, there were other reasons that led to the Civil War, and the slaves themselves joined the fight for their own independence soon enough. But the charge was led by the magnanimous Union soldiers on the battlefield and the Republicans in government. It is that decency, nobility, and compassion on which the Republican Party was built, and it's time the party rediscovers it.

Decades after slavery had been abolished and Reconstruction had taken root in the South, abolition was no longer an issue, and the Republicans had to be identified with something else. During the Roaring Twenties, the GOP settled on a different goal that was less magnanimous and chivalrous than abolishing slavery but nonetheless a beneficial one: making money, and lots of it. Long before Ronald Reagan applied trickle-down, supply-side economics in the 1980s,

Warren Harding, Calvin Coolidge, and Herbert Hoover practiced it in the 1920s first with much success, but then the stock market crash of 1929 caused the decade-long Great Depression.

It seemed as if the Republican Party—at least in terms of presidential formidability—was dead in the water. Dwight Eisenhower revived the party but governed more as a pragmatist than an ideologue. It was not until 1980 that Reagan rejuvenated the GOP's supply-side vision. The widely held perception was that those policies perpetuated in the post-Reagan era by Republicans and Democrats alike significantly contributed to the Great Recession of 2008, from which the nation has yet to rebound completely.

Republicans continue to struggle to find their footing again as they attempt to represent a political brand that a majority of Americans will embrace. Tip 4: Stop Playing It Safe! Define Your Ideals and the Votes Will Take Care of Themselves centered on the GOP's need to know itself. In doing so, Republicans also must be very mindful not to try to be Democrats.

Tip 7: Don't "Latinofy" the Message Artificially

Most Republicans, like most Americans, are not racist, as is discussed in greater detail in Tip 12: Reclaiming Race Relations. Republicans' longstanding strategy to appeal to their base—white, predominantly male Christians—was less an ideological desire to exclude than a practical approach to winning elections. Similarly, their recent realization that Latino-Americans have become a formidable voting bloc can be a dangerous proposition for them if in fact the GOP decides to "Latinofy" itself simply as a way to pander for votes.

First, Republicans who think they understand Latinos because they've read about them in a sociology book or once had a twenty-minute conversation with their gardeners are grossly mistaken if they think Latinos are a monolith. A Cuban in Miami might have entirely different values, goals, and viewpoints than a Dominican in Upper Manhattan, a Bolivian in Northern New Jersey, or a Mexican migrant worker in California. To try to capture the Latino vote would be like trying to corner the market on the white vote and to assume that fellow whites Pat Robertson and Jeanine Garofalo will vote the same way.

Second, it's an insult to Latino-Americans to assume they're in favor of sweeping amnesty for illegal aliens because many of those illegals happen to share the same ancestry they do. That is about as preposterous as saying, "Let's promise to release Ponzi schemer Bernie Madoff from prison; he's Jewish, so that will get us the Jewish vote." Immigration reform, discussed in Tip 16: Winning on Immigration, should be based on the merits, not on a cheap attempt to garner votes from an amalgam of ethnic groups.

Third, the Republicans have to learn that voters aren't idiots and that, by extension, Latino voters—a subset of all voters—specifically aren't idiots. They're not going to pull the lever in glee for the candidate who begins a speech with "Bienvenidos amigos" in a Midwestern drawl or says, "I eat tacos all the time!"

Consider the professional football player Tony Romo, who as of this writing is the starting quarterback for the Dallas Cowboys. Romo is probably most associated with being a professional football player. A very well-paid athlete, Romo is a millionaire. He's also a man, a celebrity, a husband, and a father. He's a native of California, his zodiac sign is Taurus, and he's an experienced golfer. Oh, and as the son of a Mexican-born father, Romo also happens to be a Latino.

Romo could be classified according to dozens, hundreds, and even thousands of categories. I for one have absolutely no idea where, among those thousands of categories, Romo ranks his Latino heritage. Maybe very high, maybe quite low, or maybe somewhere in between. But if Republicans begin to pigeonhole Romo along with tens of millions of other Americans into a specific and sole Latino category, they'd be on a futile wild goose chase for votes.

Also take note, Republicans: don't be like the Democrats and try to turn every Latino into a victim either. And don't be afraid to criticize a Latino who deserves criticism. Doing so only patronizes an entire group of people based on ancestral heritage. That in the long run does more harm than good.

Another important point worth mentioning is that when it comes to conservatives, Democrats and their minions take no prisoners. Just like liberals have railed against Supreme Court Justice Clarence

Thomas—his being African-American meaning nothing to them—so too would they vilify Cuban-descended Ted Cruz and Marco Rubio if it so behooved them. Therefore, if Republicans want to showcase Cruz and Rubio on their merits, that's fine. But if they think those candidates will get a Latino free pass from the left, they'd better think again.

Republicans, focus on creating a genuine message, one you truly believe regardless of how many or how few votes you think it might bring you. That way, you will attract voters in general—Latinos and others. Rediscover your dignity and credibility, and don't try to Latinofy your message artificially.

Tip 8: Support the Conservative Media Very Cautiously

The media generates much of the political divisiveness in America; some of this comes from the left, but most comes from the right. I'm not talking about mere differences of opinion but of the warlike conditions of zero tolerance and zero compromise. The conservative media is of course not inherently less fair, less ethical, or less civilized. Rather, it's vastly outnumbered, and so when it fights, it throws not peppering jabs but sweeping haymakers.

In examining the presidential election results of the past half century, seven had been won by Democrats (Kennedy in 1960, Johnson in 1964, Carter in 1976, Clinton in 1992 and 1996, and Obama in 2008 and 2012). Seven had been won by Republicans (Nixon in 1968 and 1972, Reagan in 1980 and 1984, George H. W. Bush in 1988, and George W. Bush in 2000 and 2004). Politically, then, things are about as evenly divided as they could be, but members of the mainstream media (newspapers, magazines, television, and radio) are nowhere near that fifty-fifty split. They vote Democratic overwhelmingly. Some might argue, "It's not that we're necessarily liberal, it's that the Democrats field better candidates most of the time." Exactly the point. While the nation as a whole determined that the Democrats fielded better candidates half the time and the Republicans the other half, the media, through their left-leaning lenses, evidently saw things much differently.

The *New York Times* has long been considered the newspaper of record and is among the most read in the nation. It's also among the most liberal, having become increasingly so once former publisher Arthur Ochs Sulzberger Senior turned over control to his son and namesake, Junior. The newspaper hasn't endorsed a Republican presidential candidate since the 1950s.

The other widely regarded newspaper on that same level is the *Washington Post*, which although not as rabidly ideological as the modern-day *Times*, has been left of center during most of that time. By contrast, *USA Today* is more centrist, or rather less blatantly ideological, but even though that paper enjoys a very high national circulation, it has yet to reach the level of political influence that the *Times* and the *Post* have. The *Wall Street Journal*, which has replaced *USA Today* as the most-read newspaper in America, is decidedly conservative, but its greatest influence is in the financial, not the political arena.

The evening news on television has been an information source to which Americans flock on a nightly basis since the birth of the medium itself. Free TV networks—ABC, CBS, NBC, and to some extent PBS—have dominated the airwaves even in the age of cable television. Most of their news shows lean more to the left than to the right. CNN, which for years had been the leader among the cable TV news media, is probably the most centrist, with MSNBC the most evidently left wing.

The conservatives have a stronghold on two important media outlets, however: cable news—where the Fox News Channel dominates the ratings, consistently ranking ahead of MSNBC and dwindling CNN—and conservative talk radio. The problem, however, is that because conservatives consider themselves vastly outnumbered in the media overall, they overcompensate by fighting back twice as hard and therefore appear more bitter, angry, and blindly ideological and less fair, subjective, and forthright.

Suppose we begin with the premise that the *Boston Globe*, *Time* magazine, and the *CBS Evening News*, to the extent they would veer in any direction from center, would tend to lean more left than right. Further, suppose that Fox News or the Rush Limbaugh Radio Show lean to the right. It would follow logically then that the latter group would be more critical of President Obama and the former would be more critical of his predecessor, George W. Bush. Of the two criticisms, which would be harsher, more evident, and more caustic? And which would be subtler, less abrasive, and appear more objective?

That's the point. The left-leaning media has strength in numbers and the luxury to pepper their opponents with jabs, to implement death by a thousand cuts—none of which, individually, receives much attention except for a few fringe exceptions. But the right-leaning media is decidedly bolder in its ideology, throwing wild hooks in search of that one-punch knockout and firing big, loud cannons at their opponents. Accordingly, in attempting to level the playing field, the conservative media appears as the troublemaker.

For that reason, Republicans need to stop paying attention to the media outlets that preach to the choir. They need to insist on being interviewed by more left-leaning newspapers, magazines, television shows, and radio stations. Show me a Republican who can appear on *Meet the Press* on Sunday, *Hannity* on Monday, *The Rachel Maddow Show* on Tuesday, *The O'Reilly Factor* on Wednesday, *The McNeil-Lehrer News Hour* on Thursday, *Real Time with Bill Maher* on Friday, and *The Beltway Boys* on Saturday and I'll show you a Republican who is going to win the election.

Republicans, don't be like Democrats. Don't turn a blind eye to biased reporting, pretending it doesn't exist, and don't create a double standard based on a candidate's ideological point of view.

Granted, Republicans need to support their base to a sufficient degree, and at the moment, the Fox News Channel and talk radio are their base. Nonetheless, Republicans have to work hard to be taken seriously by the broader base of the American people. Accordingly, they should continue to support the conservative media, but very cautiously.

Tip 9: Remember to Compromise

Having lived most of my life in the New York Metropolitan area and having spent most of my years as a baseball fan rooting for the Mets, I learned the difference—a generalization, of course—between Mets fans and Yankees fans. The Yankees have won more World Series titles than any other baseball team by far; many of their fans cannot accept that the Yankees don't win it every year. Mets fans by comparison typically were grateful for any Series appearance and doubly grateful for the rare win. "At least we won it in '86," they said for years until 1986 became more than a generation ago. But Yankees fans have come to accept that if it's October, the Yanks simply have to be in the World Series and they have to win it.

The Republicans have become the Yankees of politics. Unlike the Democrats—the Mets—the Republicans become irrational and inconsolable when they lose the White House. They become petty, vengeful, and uncooperative. After they lose a game, they throw a temper tantrum and turn over the board, knocking all the pieces to the floor. If they can't have any cake, they'll throw mud on it so no one else can have any either. They don't fight fire with fire; they simply fight with fire.

Consider the lunacy of the fiscal cliff, the fiasco that every year or

GRUMPY OLD PARTY | 43

two drags on seemingly endlessly and drags down the stock market and consumer confidence with it. During my college years, I worked for a retail store that sold televisions, stereos, and other electronic devices. In those days, it was common to negotiate the sales price of an item just as it is today when buying a car. After spending a couple of years in low-volume stores, where customers were few and negotiations were routine, I was transferred to a very high-volume store, where doing a good job meant keeping up with the frenetic flow of customer traffic. At that point, I decided not to waste any time pursuing the fine art of negotiation and focused instead on closing the sale as quickly as possible. Therefore, I would choose a rock-bottom price that still afforded the store some profit and open negotiations with it, which was always remarkably lower than the price tag. I'd say, "That's my best price." Here's the important part: the vast majority of my customers understood I had already compromised by making the opening offer.

Regarding the fiscal cliff, that's exactly what President Obama has done over the years. By seeking to extend the Bush tax cuts only for those making over $250,000 per year and to raise them only to the pre-Bush tax rates of the Clinton era, which were still far lower than taxes had been through most of the latter twentieth century, he had already compromised. As a Democrat reputed to be progressive, Obama could have easily opened negotiations with no extension of the Bush tax cuts; he could have opted to raise taxes above the Clinton-era rates. Instead, he slashed prices on his merchandise even before he opened the doors to the customers. Rather than meet him halfway, Republicans claim he hadn't budged at all and so neither would they.

Much of this ties in with Tip 2: Lose the Angry Tone because Republicans used their rage to breed a legion of angry supporters who refused to compromise and even made the childish claims of seceding from the Union. When they're not busy channeling their inner Rambos with guns (more on that in Tip 19: Winning on Guns), they're aspiring to be modern-day Patrick Henrys. Sure, as Obama approaches the end of his presidency, he has become more combative. But let's not forget how it all started.

Republicans might not realize that refusing to compromise is childish and downright un-American. Our nation was built on compromise so much so that it would be appropriate to call it the American States of Compromise. Folks tend to forget that our glorious Constitution, now more than 225 years old, established not our first form of government but our second. The first one, based on the Articles of Confederation, failed miserably. Remember shortly after the United States toppled Saddam Hussein's regime in Iraq how things quickly turned sour? Terrorists swarmed the region, subverting the newly installed Iraqi government's effort from taking root and routinely killing American soldiers. The situation was perilous, chaotic, untenable. To a considerable extent, it still is. Well, that's how conditions in the United States were during the first few years until the founders in their infinite wisdom got together and decided to start anew.

The second time around, they created the Constitution, considered magnificent in so many ways that many—Barack Obama included—appreciate the notion that some consider it to have been divinely inspired.[8] Had the Constitution not been written and ratified, however, it's possible the United States would have ceased to exist just a few years after its founding. It might have been reduced to an obscure reference in a history book along the lines of, "The United States was the name given to a short-lived nation started by a group of rebels that declared their independence against Great Britain and was disbanded eleven years later." The original thirteen states might have returned to be part of Great Britain, Florida might still belong to Spain, Texas to Mexico, and so on. Why were the Articles of Confederation such a failure while the Constitution was a resounding success? Compromise.

States' rights is another favorite issue among Republicans. Well, too much states' rights to the point that the federal government is powerless

---

[8] Secular leftists and Obama-bashing rightwingers sometimes refuse to believe that Obama made such a reference, but he did indeed. See *The Audacity of Hope*.

can be a bad thing. Could you imagine what would have happened when the Japanese attacked Pearl Harbor in 1941 in the absence of a strong national government? By the time the states stopped bickering about whether to declare war, when to declare it, and against whom, this great land of ours might have overtaken by the Axis Powers.

Instead, the Founders realized that for our country to be strong, individual states had to relinquish some of their power, to compromise for the greater good. Under the Constitution, states had comparatively less power than they did under the Articles—not a good outcome for states' rights purists. On the other hand, the Articles of Confederation lasted for barely seven miserable years while the Constitution is still going strong.

Compromise, then, is not only desirable; it's the very essence of America. Liberals often complain that Democrats in government often walk away from fights rather than stand by their principles. That's not what Republicans should do. Extreme agreeability can be as bad as extreme disagreeability. If the Republicans want to win back the White House, they must become the party of reason, the party of cooler heads, the party of logic. That way, they can win on compromise.

Part III: Reclaiming

The Democrats have managed to claim, or more appropriately, the Republicans have managed to cede, a number of issues that had been long-standing Republican strongholds. The next four tips focus on how to reclaim them.

Tip 10: Reclaiming Populism

The GOP was not the first party in American history to fight for the interests of ordinary folks; that distinction goes to Andrew Jackson's Democrats. But Republicans are certainly no strangers to populism. Mitt Romney's greatest difficulty in connecting with masses of Republicans, disgruntled Democrats, and swing voters in 2012 was his inability to shed the perception of being an out-of-touch rich guy. Although George W. Bush was born into no less rich and powerful a family, he seemed more like an ordinary, approachable guy – whom many people described as "a guy you'd like to have a beer with."

Though Bush's father had a "silver-spoon Republican" problem similar to Romney's, Reagan won over a whole bunch of what became known as Reagan Democrats, not least of which because of his rags-to-riches story. Before a dispirited and deflated Nixon resigned the presidency, he had won reelection by one of the most incredible landslides in history, capturing forty-nine out of fifty states. Nixon too never ceased speaking the virtues of his humble beginnings.

One of the most popular Republicans of all time, Theodore Roosevelt, famously railed against big-business monopolies. Finally, there is no better example of ensuring justice for the have-nots against the haves than that of the first and most celebrated Republican president,

Abraham Lincoln, in his intrepid and groundbreaking decision to abolish slavery. It's no coincidence that although some old-money patrician Republicans became president too, the more successful ones had definite populist streaks.

A misperception as prevalent as the one that suggests there are no populist Republicans is that Democrats usually arise from humble beginnings. Among recent Democratic presidents, Bill Clinton came from meager means, and Barack Obama, though not a child of poverty, was hardly one of privilege either. Lyndon Johnson had a humble start in life. But three Democrats whose presidencies are synonymous with helping the neediest, Carter, Kennedy, and Franklin D. Roosevelt, were hardly needy. Carter's family owned a lucrative peanut farm, and the Kennedys and the Roosevelts are among America's most-privileged families.

There is an old saying that the Republicans are the party of the rich. Why can't they be the party of the rich, the middle class, and the poor all at once? Since when has governance been reduced to a choice among policies favoring the rich, the middle class, or the poor but not all three? Why do partisan politics have to be an either/or? "You can ski in the Rocky Mountains or surf in Hawaii but not both." How about, "Some of our guests would prefer prime rib, others chicken, and others fish. Let's serve all three."?

A simple way to satisfy all Americans regardless of their economic situations is to keep corporate taxes extremely low provided that corporations hire American workers. That creates wealth for the haves, the have-nots, and those in between all at once. Another would be to reward businesses with tax incentives and preferred status in government bidding contracts based on how narrow the gaps were between their top, middle, and bottom earners. Give the perks to the company whose CEO makes just 200 times as much as one of the janitors, not 5,000 times as much.

The United States is not a handful of lords commanding millions of serfs. It's far deeper than a bunch of wealthy barons voting for nothing but the ability to retain as much of their fortunes as possible and ungrateful welfare recipients who believe it's their constitutional right and their lot in life to be taken care of by the government.

Between those two extremes is a huge majority comprising hardworking Americans who for one reason or another are at various points along the financial independence scale. Some of them own small businesses or aspire to do so, but not all do, and not all want to.

An important point for Republicans to realize is that not everyone's version of the American dream is to own a business or a home. Some folks are perfectly happy working for someone else. They don't mind following orders; they just want fewer headaches. Similarly, some folks don't care about owning a home. Sure, it would be nice, but they don't want to have to deal with the responsibilities that go with it. Instead, they can just pick up the phone and call the superintendent or the landlord when the sink is clogged or when the window breaks. Ironically, Republicans often complain that Democrats like to tell people what to do, but the GOP is guilty of that too in its thinking that all Americans have the same definitions of happiness and success.

There's certainly nothing wrong with making millions or even billions as long as the money is earned honestly. There's nothing wrong with inheriting wealth. The most natural and arguably the most just way for society to function is a meritorious one: you reap what you sow. Aaron Rodgers will earn more money than his football team's third-string quarterback. Madonna will receive a higher percentage of the proceeds from a live concert or from album sales than her drummer will. And the pizza maker who starts work earlier and goes home later than his competitor across the street will earn more. That's fair. A company's CEO making 200 times as much as its janitor is fair, too, but when the CEO makes 5,000 times as much, that becomes outrageous.

The Republicans don't have to be poor to win elections or even suggest that the poor and the middle class are any more important than the wealthy. They shouldn't be like Democrats in terms of filling their campaign speeches with as many hard-luck stories as possible.

There's nothing wrong with making a buck or even lots of bucks, and the Republicans should continue to say that.

On the other hand, if they suggest, as Romney did, that students who have a hard time paying for college ought to borrow the money from their parents, that will perpetuate the stereotype of Republicans being woefully out of touch. To reclaim the White House, the Republicans have to reclaim populism.

Tip 11: Reclaiming Patriotism

The Democrats have had a stronghold on populism on and off since their launching by the father of American populism himself, Andrew Jackson, as a major political party. Patriotism, however, has been a Republican mainstay since Ronald Reagan put his emblem on it and George W. Bush had it laminated. But in one fell swoop, Barack Obama took it back, despite what his detractors will tell you, and suddenly, seemingly overnight, the Democrats became the party of patriotism.

Obama's vice president, Joe Biden, said it best when he described what the Democrats' bumper sticker ought to say: General Motors is alive and Osama bin Laden is dead. That in a nutshell captures how and why the Democrats snatched patriotism from the Republicans' clutches.

General Motors symbolizes America's economic prowess. For years, it was pro-business Republicans who said, "What's good for General Motors is good for the country." The American auto industry in general is an example of American ingenuity and why the entire world has the United States to thank for no longer having to travel on horseback. And yet, that same Republican Party turned its back on General Motors when that company faced bankruptcy, and they chastised and ridiculed Obama for wanting to step in and save the day. But save the day he did, and General Motors experienced a level of success (despite overhype) it hadn't seen in a long time. American cars and the American workers who built them had been saved.

That's patriotism the Republicans can reclaim if they focus on supporting the American worker. Right or wrong, there was a widely held belief that 2012 Republican nominee Mitt Romney would measure economic growth and success strictly by looking at collective profit—how many additional billions American corporations would amass when lowering their overhead by outsourcing American jobs to low-wage-paying nations—and ignoring the fact that those beneath the upper economic echelon wouldn't share in the spoils. That he of all people in 2015, while mulling over whether to run for president again, had the audacity to criticize the current economic recovery as one skewed toward favoring the rich is astounding because the obvious reaction should have been, why wasn't he saying any of that in 2012?

Republicans need to seize the moral high ground and compel corporations—shame them, actually—into putting patriotism above profit. Sure, they can still make a buck, but they ought to do so by staying right here in the good ol' USA rather than outsourcing production to the lands of cheap labor.

Another Republican of yore worth emulating is Senator Arthur Vandenberg, who said, "Politics stops at the water's edge," meaning that Americans shouldn't argue among themselves, particularly in Congress, when it comes to foreign affairs. Family patriarch Don Vito Corleone in the movie *The Godfather* admonished his firstborn, Sonny—the characters played brilliantly by Marlon Brando and James Caan respectively—for publicly displaying his skepticism about a decision his father had made: "What's the matter with you? ... Never tell anybody outside the family what you're thinking again." Today's Republicans, however, seem not to have learned from either example. They try to tear down Obama at every turn, purportedly for the good of the country, when in fact they're just panhandling for votes. That's not patriotism.

Another well-known saying is that elections have consequences.

Barack Obama won in 2008. He won again in 2012. He's the president of the United States. Get over it, Republicans, and stop second-guessing him all the time. There's a difference between respectful dissent and scathing disdain. Listen to Senator Vandenberg and Don Corleone.

Another reason why the Republicans have relinquished their supremacy on patriotism is due to the growing perception of how poorly they treat veterans of the US armed forces. Stories of forgotten, unemployed, destitute, and medically undertreated veterans abound, and Democrats appear more patriotic when they are the ones fighting for veterans' rights. If Republicans would clearly outperform Democrats when it comes to veterans' issues, they would recapture that all-important constituency.

The vast majority of elected officials in both parties—if not the entire lot of them—deeply love the United States. There's a troublesome perception, however, that as of late, the Republicans' love of country is rooted in the notion of looking out for number one, with number one being oneself, America simply providing the guarantee that no one will stand in the way.

It is not, though, that Republicans should be like Democrats in their patriotism. They should not apologize for American exceptionalism or justify other nations' actions vis-à-vis their counterparts around the world by some all-encompassing notion of moral relativism.

Nonetheless, if the GOP is serious about winning the White House anytime soon, it must make the greater good a higher priority than number one. Then it truly can reclaim patriotism.

Tip 12: Reclaiming Race Relations

As explained in Tip 7: Don't "Latinofy" the Message Artificially, most Americans are not racist, and most Republicans aren't either. Most of the more than 59 million votes cast against Barack Obama in the 2012 election had nothing to do with race, but many did. It's nearly impossible of course to guess how many racists are out there considering that most people wouldn't readily admit it. But let's be generous and say 99 percent of the votes against Obama had nothing to do with race. That would mean 1 percent—approximately 600,000—didn't vote for Obama because he is African-American. Today, such a high number is frightening and embarrassing.

To the extent there are racists in the Republican Party or in its unofficial offshoot, the Tea Party, Republicans need to be vocal about denouncing racism. It's one thing to pay lip service to something but another to condemn it totally. It's that latter frame of mind in which all Republicans need to place themselves to reclaim credibility. Racists shouldn't be welcome in any political party, least of all in the party that abolished slavery. Exerting the same intensity with which they would hunt down terrorists, or better yet, any hint of a tax hike, Republicans need to track down racists and expunge them from their ranks.

Republicans also need to understand that though most Americans don't have a problem with Obama's race to the extent that they would, say, wish him harm, they might be more prone to believe wild rumors that he is a secret Muslim, for instance, than they would about a white president such as George W. Bush. "Hmmm, he *does* have a strange name—Barack Hussein Obama—and he *was* raised in Indonesia. That much we know … but I heard he was really born in Kenya too" might be the reasoning. And though that may not qualify as actual racism—it's more like an inaccurate race-based stereotype, and there is a difference—it's nonetheless a problem Republicans ought to be aware of. It's unacceptable for Republicans to say, "I'm not the one saying these things, and I'm not personally responsible for those who do, but if it means fewer votes for Obama and more votes for our candidate, well, I'm not going to stand in the way of that."

During the 2008 campaign, a woman told John McCain that she heard Obama was "an Arab." McCain quickly stopped her. "No ma'am. He's a decent family man and citizen that I just happen to have fundamental disagreements with on issues." The woman apparently hadn't been listening carefully when a few seconds earlier, McCain had made the following remarks: "First of all, I'd want to be president of the United States and obviously I do not want Senator Obama to be. But I have to tell you … he is a decent person that you do not have to be scared [of] as president of the United States." After some boos and exasperated loud sighs from the bloodthirsty crowd, McCain continued, "Now look. If I didn't think that I wouldn't be one heck of a lot *better* president, I wouldn't be running, okay? And that's the point. That's the point."

That was one of the finest moments in modern-day presidential campaigning. McCain put his head right into the lion's mouth and effectively said, "Stop all this nonsense!" To a lesser extent, the 2012 GOP nominee, Mitt Romney, also showed signs of decency toward that same Democratic opponent. Consistently, Romney referred to Obama as a nice guy who just wasn't doing a good enough job as president.

No good deed goes unpunished. Some on the left used the

opportunity to twist those words around in an attempt to make McCain and Romney, both of whom in that instance had taken the high road, look bad. Alec Baldwin chastised McCain for responding that Obama was a decent family man to the statement that he was an Arab as follows: "Does that mean an Arab *wouldn't* be a good family man?" Leave it to Alec Baldwin to view a noble gesture through a prism laden with partisan venom. Bill Maher, too, on whose show *Real Time* Baldwin made those comments in 2008, twisted Romney's words around in 2012, suggesting that Republicans who said Obama was a nice guy who "tried" were patronizing him because he was African-American, implying that "Oh, the black guy *tried*, but you know, he just can't measure up to a white man's job."

Republicans, don't take the bait. Don't flatly deny that racism exists just because the Democrats overstate its prevalence. Instead, win back the moral high road and let the left hoard the market on cheap shots.

Republicans will reclaim race relations only when they become comfortable in being truly colorblind. White liberals are infamous for their claim of understanding the plight that persons of color experience. Guilty, self-loathing, white liberals in particular are the ones who coddle them. Though these coddlers are well intentioned, they do more harm by patronizing those they wish to help.

Republicans, on the other hand, can prove themselves the superior party on any race issue by treating all people the same. Truly the same. That means in terms of praise and condemnation as applicable. Most people of every race in turn will respect that kind of evenhanded treatment, and the Republicans will reclaim the issue of race relations.

Tip 13: Reclaiming National Security

Of all the Republican strongholds Democrats have taken possession of, their most amazing heist is the issue of national security. When Reagan won the White House in a landslide in 1980, American morale was at a dismally low level because fifty-four Americans had been held hostage by a new extremist regime in Iran. The mighty United States had been humiliated on the world stage, but from the very moment Reagan was inaugurated, his first dose of good news to the American people—and a whopping dose it was—was to announce the hostages had been released. From that point on, Republicans were the standard bearer of America's strength until Obama stepped in to lead the Democrats.

Much to the chagrin of his leftmost supporters, Obama proved early on that he was no dove. He began using Special Forces to combat terrorism, culminating in the killing of Osama bin Laden. The decision involved in that daring mission—one that had it backfired could have cost him tremendous backlash and possibly reelection—was his alone. Obama continued construction of a fence along America's southern border, accelerated deportation of illegal alien felons, and doubled down on the war in Afghanistan. He even retained President Bush's top brass, Defense Secretary Robert Gates and General David Petraeus (the latter, who until an unfortunate personal scandal caused him to fall from grace, had been America's most beloved military figure since Colin Powell).

Best of all, Obama was able to enjoy unfettered use of the military without the usual litany of "He lied, kids died" protests because he was a Democrat. Sometimes, presidents get a pass simply by virtue of their political party and reputation. Nixon's celebrated anticommunist image didn't suffer when he visited Communist China in 1971. Had his Democratic opponent, Hubert Humphrey, won the 1968 election and gone to China, he would have been politically destroyed.

Similarly, Obama didn't have to worry about tarnishing his image of being a champion of human rights and social justice when he took drone lobbing into terrorist cells to new levels—after all, he had already won the Nobel Peace Prize after only eight months as president and had been nominated for it within a few days of taking office.

None of this is to blame Obama. Rather, it's to point out that when Republicans criticize Obama on matters of national security and his way appears to be the right way, they wind up on the wrong side of history and on the wrong side of national security. Republicans need to honor the good work the president has done but promise to do better.

Granted, particularly in his second term, Obama has suffered on the world stage. But Republicans had been bashing him long before that. Instead, they should acknowledge Obama's successes but add that even if he's doing a good job at times, America is a great country whose president must do a great job.

When it comes to Iran, the Republicans are right to call for even more crippling, swift, and overwhelming sanctions. The strategy should be proactive. They are right to criticize any nuclear agreement that's too giving and forgiving. But it should be a constructive, solutions-centered criticism, not one based on, "If Obama's for it, we're against it."

Closely tied to national security interests is energy independence. We'll discuss how to obtain energy independence in more detail in Tip 15: Winning on Energy Independence. For now, let's agree that achieving energy independence would likely render rogue, oil-rich nations such as Iran and nationless gangs of terrorists utterly irrelevant to the United States and ultimately to the entire world.

Also critical to reducing other potentially threatening nations to irrelevance is improving the Strategic Defense Initiative (SDI) that Reagan not only talked about but that also ultimately caused the Soviet Union to fold. Liberals derided Reagan's plan as star-wars stuff, which of course was a misnomer because it implied that SDI was an aggressive measure when nothing could have been more peaceful. SDI doesn't involve harming the hair on a single person's head or destroying even one square inch of anyone's land. The only damage it causes is to an incoming missile, which it intercepts and obliterates. Once SDI is perfected, any nuclear weapon aimed at the United States might as well be made of cotton candy.

As for the naysayers who say SDI cannot be achieved, it was no closer to having been achieved twenty-five years ago when Reagan won the Cold War by bringing it up in conversation. If the Wright Brothers had listened to the doubters—not least of which was the *New York Times*, which in an editorial suggested it would take one to ten million years to develop a machine that could fly—it would still take us days, not hours, to travel across the country or around the world.[9]

Republicans have a golden opportunity to praise Obama for the good he has done in terms of foreign policy but to highlight how they could do better—much better. Unlike the Democrats, Republicans must continue to emphasize that America is in the unique position to remain the leader of the free world. Not the sole arbiter of the free world, mind you, but the premier nation among many, leading the way to establish global safety and well-being at least to the extent necessary to ensure long-term national security at home.

On the other hand, the GOP must make sure not to repeat its mistakes and get trapped in the vast military-industrial complex President Eisenhower warned about so long ago. But they must not,

---

[9] "Flying Machines Which Do Not Fly," Editorial, *New York Times*, October 9, 1903.

as Democrats do, utter the words "We can't afford to go to war" because war should never be an economic decision. We are the greatest superpower in the history of the world; if we have to go to war, then go to war we shall, and money will be no object.

War, however, should always be the last resort even if we were rolling in so much money that we didn't know where to spend it. Finally, war should be quick, bold, overwhelming, and decisive; no more quagmires. As one of the most celebrated Republican presidents, Theodore Roosevelt, said, "Speak softly, but carry a big stick." A presidential descendant of his several decades later, Reagan—much celebrated in his own right—put it even more simply: "Peace through strength."

Americans must feel a sense of comfort with the GOP steering the ship. Once that happens, the Republicans will reclaim national security.

Top: Dwight D. Eisenhower (Dwight D. Eisenhower
Presidential Library & Museum)
Bottom: Andrew Jackson

When Republicans say they wouldn't raise taxes under any circumstances, they sound eminently unreasonable. Keep in mind that the top rate under immensely popular Republican President Dwight Eisenhower was 92 percent!

As for deficit spending and debt accumulation, both parties are plenty guilty. Only one president in the history of our country ever paid off the country's debt: Andrew Jackson (who, by the way, was a Democrat).

Top: America's growing wealth gap
Bottom: A "Made in the USA" sign

After having blasted Candidate Obama in 2008 for wanting to "spread the wealth," Republicans sound quite disingenuous nowadays as they suddenly raise concerns about America's growing wealth gap. Spreading the wealth is not an absolute yes or no concept; it's just a matter of extent.

A related topic is the American worker: our nation is not at its best when a "good economy" means only the big corporations profit, and do so by hiring cheap labor overseas instead of their fellow Americans at home.

Top: A nativity scene
Bottom: Celebrating Diwali

America was not founded as a Christian nation, as some in the GOP purport, but it certainly is one now. An overwhelming 73 percent of Americans identify themselves with that religion. The Constitution didn't prohibit religious displays on public property; it merely allowed for any religious point of view to be represented. So a school can have a Merry Christmas sign next to, say, one that reads, "Happy Diwali" (a Hindu religious festival of lights).

Top: Guns and the Second Amendment
Bottom: Immigration to the United States

The Founding Fathers fully intended for individuals to keep and bear arms long before the Second Amendment was written. But that right, like any other, is not limitless.

As for immigration, while the debate continues about what to do with illegal aliens currently here, how about zero tolerance for any future ones coming in illegally? Can't everyone agree on that?

Part IV: Winning

Other key issues are up for grabs. If the Republicans follow the final seven tips, they can win on those issues and win back the White House.

Tip 14: Winning on Taxes

Winning on taxes is closely related to Tip 10: Reclaiming Populism. It begins with a mutual absurdity shared by both major parties—that raising taxes slightly on a tiny percentage of the population will make a hill of beans' worth of difference.

Early in 2001, as the nation enjoyed a brief respite from deficit spending and created a surplus—though a recession had begun to fester even before he took office—President George W. Bush imposed tax cuts across the board, which to this day are referred to as the Bush tax cuts. Ever since Bush left office in January 2009, the Democrats and Republicans have debated whether to make those tax cuts permanent or let them expire, as Congress had originally provided when it enacted them.

The Democrats have made it an issue of fairness that the wealthy should pay their fair share of the mounting debt, and they maintain that even modest tax hikes would go a long way toward creating new revenue. The Republicans, on the other hand, believe that particularly during a sluggish economy, even the mere whiff of a tax increase would stifle any momentum and thrust us back into another recession.

If the percentage of the taxpayers or the tax hikes themselves were significant, the debate would be substantive. However, the recent change in income tax rates is so minor that debating it is like arguing that a change in temperature of one degree would result in a frost or a heat wave.

Republicans ought to end this ludicrous gamesmanship predicated on their bitter frustration because they lost to Obama twice and lost the popular vote in five out of the last six presidential elections; they should start acting more like the man they want to emulate but have no clue what he was really all about: Ronald Reagan. They need a spokesperson with Reagan's charisma, even just a fraction of it, to come up with a simple and bold tax plan and stick to it.

In the 2012 Republican primaries, Herman Cain made a mockery out of career politicians by coming up with his 9–9–9 plan, a tax of 9 percent on income, 9 percent on sales of new goods, and 9 percent on corporations. Whether it would have been feasible is another matter; the point is he said it, and people listened.

Republicans might consider a national sales tax that would replace rather than supplement the IRS. That way, workers who make $500 per week keep $500 per week. Those who make $1,000 per week keep $1,000 per week. Simple as that. Then, they can come up with the right percentage the tax should to be to account for continued spending, proper savings, and economic stability. Perhaps it should be phased in over ten years as follows.

Year	Percentage of Taxes Based on Sales	Percentage of Taxes Based on Income
1	10%	90%
2	20%	80%
3	30%	70%
4	40%	60%
5	50%	50%
6	60%	40%
7	70%	30%
8	80%	20%
9	90%	10%
10	100%	0%

Currently, Americans pay income tax but not federal sales tax. Under this plan, if you think of their income tax payment as a ten-slice pizza pie, each year, a slice would be taken away from income tax and paid in sales tax until after ten years, the only tax Americans would pay would be a sales tax; income tax would be zero. That way, the change would be gradual. Basic necessities (bread, toothpaste, and so on) would be tax exempt, while luxury items (diamonds and caviar) would be taxed at a higher rate.

Next, there is the corporate tax to consider. Democrats often think that corporations profit too much as it is, so the last thing they want to do is consider the Republicans' proposal to cut corporate taxes even more to bolster economic growth. How about a step in between? Cut taxes for those corporations that pledge to keep their production in the United States. That would be their reward for putting country first, as we discussed in Tip 10: Reclaiming Patriotism.

Mitt Romney did raise a good point during the 2012 presidential campaign when he proposed a revenue-neutral tax reduction whereby tax rates would be lowered but loopholes would close. That's something akin to the flatter, fairer tax for which George W. Bush campaigned in 2000 in the general election after having outdueled his Republican primary opponents, including Steve Forbes, whose campaign focused on a flat tax.

Republicans' main problem is that they create a perception that their top priority is to make sure folks who make lots of money get to keep as much of it as possible. A close second is that they don't seem particularly interested in the ever-expanding wealth gap. Would there ever be a time in their estimation when the words *spread the wealth* would be acceptable to them? What if 99 percent of the wealth in this country was not controlled by, say, 1 percent of the population, but only fifty people, or ten, or just one? When would they say enough is enough? Also, would there ever be a time when they might say taxes had come down far enough or were so low that we needed to raise them? How far would the income tax rates have to fall without being replaced by any other kind of tax for them to say that? Twenty percent? Ten? Five? Two?

Let's stay with that hypothetical for another moment. If the income tax rate was 2 percent, even for multimillionaires, would Republicans concede that such a rate was too low? Would they dare suggest that it be raised even to 10 percent? If the answer is no, then the GOP, despite some relapse victories here and there, is on its way to extinction. If the answer is yes, the Republicans have a communication problem because too many Americans don't believe the GOP has any compassion for anyone other than the very rich.

Do Republicans really believe that raising taxes by a nominal amount would cause wealthy folks to keep their money in their mattresses and decide not to expand their businesses? Either they believe that—which means they need to understand human behavior a lot better than they do—or they don't believe it, which means the perception is true and they're merely pandering to their sugar-daddy benefactors.

Republicans certainly must not be Democrats about this. They must hold the line on the pitfalls of runaway taxation. They must also continue to maintain—and they are absolutely correct in doing so—that spending cuts at this point would be a far more effective way to achieve deficit reduction and long-term economic stability than would tax increases.

No matter what tax reform approach the Republicans adopt, it's bound to be better than what we have in place. They have a great opportunity to regain the issue that catapulted Reagan conservatism as America's mainstream political movement three decades ago. To win back the White House, Republicans must win on taxes.

Tip 15: Winning on Energy Independence

Energy independence is a no-brainer issue on which Republicans can win and to some extent bring along those on the left who think Obama and most other Democrats are too indifferent when it comes to the environment. The strategy is three-pronged: "Drill, baby, drill" is part of it, but also "Buy, baby, buy" and "Green, baby, green." The "Drill, baby, drill" point of view, made famous during the 2008 presidential campaign, particularly by GOP vice presidential nominee Sarah Palin, included drilling in parts of Palin's Alaska, in various other parts of the United States, and offshore.

Environmentalists and conservationists were outraged; they demanded more green energy instead. The mistake Republicans made was to push for more drilling without addressing the need to invest in alternatives. One of those other opportunities is for the United States to buy all the oil it can afford. If earth is running out of oil, why not stockpile it right now? That's where "Buy, baby, buy" comes in. With those two prongs in place, Republicans should embrace green energy even more loudly than Democrats do.

By implementing all three policies at once, the United States will be on the fast track to energy independence, which ultimately would render other oil-producing countries irrelevant—particularly those that don't want to play by the same rules as the United States and the other countries around the world that are interested in peace.

One way to get the American people onboard is to change the terminology. Recently, the Democrats were able to do that to some extent by renaming "global warming," their primary environmental concern, as "climate change." Some observers astutely pointed out that global warming didn't sound alarming; it sounded cozy. Climate change sounds more serious, and more important, it's not limited to warming. It includes cooling, more hurricanes, tornados, tsunamis—any kind of climatic change. Similarly, the Republicans need to rebrand energy independence and call it the energy race.

Americans love a good race. The arms race, the space race—you name it. Create a race and they'll be onboard. The energy race would be a race to drill, a race to buy, and a race to go green. It would no longer be about oil versus the environment, conservation versus expansion. It would be a race, and Americans would stand behind the party that leads the way. The Republicans need to leapfrog over the Democrats on this issue and ride it all the way to the White House. Unlike the Democrats, they need to add excitement to the equation, excitement that will be instrumental in their chances of winning at the polls by winning on energy independence.

Tip 16: Winning on Immigration

The GOP has fumbled the ball on a number of issues but probably on none as much as it has on immigration. Both major parties are woefully inept, even downright spineless, when it comes to dealing with that notoriously named third-rail issue. As usual, the concern is self-serving. As covered in Tip 7: Don't "Latinofy" the Message Artificially, Republicans are concerned that the enormous Latin American community will shun them if they don't bend over backward to champion the rights of all aliens whether legal or illegal.

Then there's the less-spoken reason, cheap labor. Do American business owners want all that cheap labor to dry up? You know, the sub-minimum-wage, off-the-books aliens who wash dishes in restaurants, fix roofs, mow lawns, and pick fruit? The kind who will rent an apartment, pay the rent on time every month, and never complain when the sink is clogged or the refrigerator door doesn't close properly? Most important, is the American economy really ready to take such a hit?

As for the Democrats, many of them hope that turning illegal aliens into US citizens will create millions of new constituents who will vote Democratic, thereby establishing that party as the overwhelmingly dominant one. Then there are those who are uncomfortable with America's Eurocentric heritage and want to impose social engineering to ensure other continents of the world are better represented in terms of the American population even if it means granting amnesty to millions of illegals.

For Republicans to win on immigration, they need to first stop with all the political correctness. There is no such thing as an illegal immigrant or an undocumented immigrant. By definition, an immigrant is someone who has attained legal immigration status (first as a legal permanent resident and subsequently as a naturalized US citizen). Moreover, anyone currently in the United States who is not a citizen is an alien. That's the legal terminology though much of the media and politicians ignore that. Legal permanent residents and legal nonimmigrants (e.g., student visa holders) are legal aliens, and those who entered or remained in the United States without permission are illegal aliens.

Next, Republicans have to realize the vast majority of illegal aliens aren't terrorists or druglords. Just as most American-born folks are good, law-abiding people, so are most illegal aliens. Of course, simply by being illegal, they're breaking the law, but otherwise, they make positive contributions to society through their hard work, their paying of taxes, and their following most if not all other laws. The main problem with illegal immigration is not terrorism and drug trafficking (nonetheless, neither of those problems should be ignored either).

Next, Republicans must understand that illegal immigration is not the only problem. Unrestricted legal immigration can have a negative impact on the economy. Virgil Goode, the Constitution Party's presidential nominee in 2012, proposed a moratorium on most immigration visas until unemployment in the United States fell below 5 percent. As did most non-major-party presidential candidates, Goode scrambled for even a fraction of 1 percent of the total vote. He finished fifth overall, with about 120,000 votes out of more than 128 million. Unfortunately, it's often only smaller-party candidates or unconventional major-party candidates seeking attention who take bold stands such as Goode's.

Democratic and Republican Party general election nominees, by contrast, are usually gun-shy when it comes to upsetting the apple cart, so they refrain from making statements that might cost them votes with any particular group. If the Republicans can bring themselves to address the issue of legal immigration too instead of a vague reference to illegal immigration only, that would go a long way toward meaningful immigration reform.[10]

Finally, the Republicans must identify the two major components of dealing with illegal aliens: what to do with those already here, and how to stop more from coming. If they concentrated more on tackling the second problem, more folks would begin to care less about the first. Even the most ardent nativists care less about how many illegal aliens are already here than about how many more are likely to come.

The immigration fence has become the symbol of the Republican plan and has even been adopted and implemented by President Obama (yet another example of how he's not the ultraliberal his opponents make him out to be). But the fence along the US border with Mexico is only one of the many components necessary to combat illegal immigration; there's also the border with Canada to consider. While many Americans think of desperate Mexicans sneaking into our nation in the middle of the night, it's foolhardy to think the same isn't being done from Canada. Granted, the problem from the north is not quite as severe. Unlike Mexico (adjacent to South America), Canada doesn't flow into an entire continent that contains millions of aspiring US migrants willing to travel to the US border and cross it illegally. Second, Canadians are less likely to be so unsatisfied with their standard of living that they will leave their country in the first place. That said, it's important to keep in mind that even with all its problems, the United States remains the country in which more people around the world—Canada included— would like to live than in any other.

---

[10] That Donald Trump did so as a Republican presidential candidate is truly groundbreaking in modern times. Perhaps it has to do with the fact that he is not a career politician, and so he is less inclined to play it safe.

Border jumping aside, illegal aliens also acquire that status by remaining in the United States beyond their allotted time. Some come here legally but overstay their time and become illegal. Combatting illegal immigration, then, also depends on a much better system of monitoring those who are granted legal nonimmigrant (temporary) status such as visitors, students, and temporary workers. There are not nearly enough federal agents available to apprehend those who simply choose not to leave by their deadlines.

One way to ensure more-effective monitoring is to require that any nonimmigrant for however brief a visit to the United States must be sponsored by an American citizen. That citizen has to take full responsibility—including civil liability—if the alien he or she sponsors fails to leave the United States on time. If American citizen John wants his niece Maria, who is from a foreign country, to visit him, John needs to sponsor Maria. If Maria fails to leave the United States by the agreed-upon date on her nonimmigrant visa, John must pay a hefty fine. It will all boil down to whether John trusts his niece to do the right thing. Of course, if John willingly and knowingly assists Maria in violating immigration laws, he must be subject to criminal liability too.

Similarly, employers should undertake the same responsibility for their nonimmigrant temporary workers and colleges for their foreign students. Colleges, after all, often charge foreign students double tuition, so they have plenty of money at risk in that situation. Next, there needs to be more-effective monitoring of employers who hire illegal aliens, and it should extend to homeowners who hire roofers, plumbers, and gardeners and those who rent apartments.

The Republican Party should stand up and fight for the authority of state and local police to assist in immigration law enforcement. The argument advanced by President Obama and the Democrats and supported by the US Supreme Court, that the enforcement of immigration law rests with the federal government exclusively, is fallacious. War and treason are acts of a federal scope too, so does that mean if someone in town attempts to build a nuclear bomb or tries to shoot the president, the local police who are nearby ought to stand by idly with fingers crossed and hope federal authorities will arrive in time to handle the situation?

Granted, individual states cannot create their own laws regarding immigration. But to prohibit local law enforcement from preserving law and order because of some ill-conceived notion that they were encroaching on federal turf would be as preposterous as a postal worker being prohibited from extinguishing a fire that ignited along his or her route because it was the fire department's job.

The next question is what to do with the illegal aliens already here. Consider this bold, simple, and transformational plan.

1. Deport all illegal aliens convicted of felonies immediately and permanently, period.

2. Provide a track to legal status—one for which they must work hard—to all illegal aliens who were brought to the United States under age eighteen by one or more adults (e.g., family members).

3. Require intense civil service obligations from and hefty fines on illegal aliens who haven't committed felonies but came here illegally of their own volition as adults. If they want to become Americans, let them go to the end of the line, behind the folks who are going through the process legally.

4. None of that should take effect until there is a zero-tolerance plan in place to prevent anyone else from coming or remaining here illegally.

Of course, there are special situations. Consider an illegal alien who is eighty-five and has been in the United States for decades, has paid Social Security and income taxes all those years, has never broken the law otherwise, has children and grandchildren here, and so forth.

Or an illegal alien who fled to the United States to escape having his or her head chopped off by a fundamentalist terrorist back home. Or an illegal alien who is very ill and has only a few months to live whose deportation would be inhumane. Special cases can be treated fairly and compassionately via special laws such as congressional acts. In any case, they would involve only a small fraction of the entire illegal alien population. These steps may not resolve the total illegal alien problem in the United States, but they would be a very good start.

Republicans must not be afraid to stand up for these changes. They must not be weak-kneed, as many Democrats are, and fear the race card. None of this has anything to do with racism or xenophobia. If racists and xenophobes support these measures, shame on them, not on the measures. It is a matter of law and order; it's compassionate yet bold. If Republicans adopt this position, they can and will win on immigration.

Tip 17: Winning on Religion

Relentless, uncompromising fundamentalism extends beyond politics into religion and spirituality. On the one hand are the theist fundamentalists who are convinced there is a god and they know exactly what that god wants and how that god wants everyone to behave. They believe anyone who doesn't follow their version of theology to the letter will incur the creator's wrath and burn in hell. Such fundamentalists are found handily in Judaism and Islam, but in America, they are most prevalent in Christianity—which makes sense, considering that 73 percent of Americans are Christian.

The counterparts to those rigid theists are the atheist fundamentalists. They are convinced that the billions upon billions of people throughout the world who have believed in God throughout the centuries are foolish, gullible, wishful thinkers, and only atheists are smart, observant, and courageous enough to understand there really is no god. Their fundamentalism becomes evident when they become irate and utterly inconsolable at the mere mention of a supreme being. Much as the fundamentalists who want the United States to be an unabashedly Christian nation, atheists won't rest until Jesus is relegated to the status of Santa Claus and the Easter Bunny.

There are, of course, plenty of theists and atheists who are enlightened enough and secure enough in their beliefs to respect alternative points of view and remain open to the possibility that they might be wrong. Republicans need to be like them, not like the fundamentalists. A rational thinker can agree more with another rational thinker who has a different point of view than with a fundamentalist who has the same point of view.

As any rational thinker knows, a spiritual journey is dynamic. It can change at any moment, take unpredictable forms, and travel in unimaginable directions. Some who are unwavering in their beliefs believe what they profess at their core, whereas others merely want to convince themselves of that. The latter are much like the person who falls in love after every first date, posts glowing odes and promises of eternal devotion to the object of his or her affection on Facebook, and starts all over again a week later with someone else.

Similarly, some serious scholars of theology have attended seminary for the better part of their adult lives and have read countless religious treatises. Then there are those who wake up drunk under a van, wonder how they got there, realize they've had enough, grab a free meal from a soup kitchen where Scripture is being quoted, and pick up a Bible. A week later, they grant themselves the title of minister or reverend and open up their own churches to preach the good news.

The Republican Party can embrace whichever of those folks it wants as long as it remains open-minded. For instance, when Republicans proclaim that God doesn't condone abortion, homosexuality, or premarital sex and base those proclamations on the Bible, they may not realize that others consider the Bible to be a radical, Johnny-come-lately departure from original Christianity and even question the use of the word *God* to refer to the heavenly father as opposed to the more original Yahuah or Yahweh.

Others proclaim that America is a Christian nation, not recognizing that many of the Founding Fathers—most notably Thomas Jefferson, author of the Jefferson Bible, which essentially removed any of the miracles performed by Jesus Christ as well as the Resurrection—were Deists. Deists are a broad range of theists who don't necessarily derive their belief in God from the Bible or from any church or religious denomination.

Republicans need to tone down their religious rhetoric to save making fools of themselves when scrutinized by serious scholars of theology and to prevent droves of potential voters from being turned off by their intolerance. On the other hand, the GOP can win on religion by being different from the politically correct Democrats by reminding Americans that in this country we have freedom of religion, not freedom from religion. As they shun their own fundamentalism, Republicans will have more credibility in pointing out the dangers of atheist fundamentalists, and they must be vigilant in doing so. Republicans must point out that it's fine for someone to choose not to believe in God but it's not good to get into a tizzy because the words *under God* appear in the Pledge of Allegiance.

The overwhelming majority of Americans identify themselves as Christians. If America didn't begin as a Christian nation, it certainly has become one. Most Americans—including Christians, non-Christians, agnostics, and atheists—have no problem with anyone saying, "Merry Christmas." It's absurd, as Republicans must point out, for the vast majority of Americans to change their ways for what is known in law as "the oversensitive plaintiff." To carry that line of thinking to its preposterous conclusion, we shouldn't celebrate Valentine's Day, St. Patrick's Day, Thanksgiving Day, or Halloween because all those holidays have some sort of religious connotation.

Following that logic, let's not even ask anyone, "What's your sign?" because astrology will offend the science-only sense of the fundamentalist atheist. Beauty contests, sporting events, even chess games all offend some minority fringe group's sensibilities. Shall we simply do away with all those too? If Republicans raise these points while distancing themselves from fundamentalism within their own ranks, they can win on religion.

Tip 18: Winning on Education

Several years ago, I was a dean at a college in New York City. One of my responsibilities for a while was direct supervision of the math department. Many of our students—mirroring their counterparts across the country—were weak in basic math skills, having been pushed through a system of public education without having mastered the rudimentary knowledge necessary to advance to higher grades. (More on that later.)

We explored many options to improve our students' math aptitude, including purchasing advanced-learning tools and implementing math across the curriculum. For example, history teachers might say, "the United States became a nation in 1776, and the Civil War began in 1861. How many years later was that?" We debated creating smaller, aesthetically pleasing classes and sending math instructors to professional development conferences.

All that sounded good in theory. But my best math instructor, the one who turned out the best-performing students semester after semester based on college-wide, objective testing criteria, didn't send any students to use the state-of-the-art learning tools, didn't collaborate with instructors in other disciplines to instill math across the curriculum, and didn't attend any conferences. He used nothing but chalk and a blackboard in a room in which forty or so students were crammed. The reason he was so successful, as I quickly discovered, was because he knew how to teach.

Teaching involves not only skill but also a great deal of talent. If we are handed Hank Aaron's bat, could we hit over 750 home runs? Or Leonard Da Vinci's paintbrush—could we paint the *Mona Lisa*? What about William Shakespeare's pen—could we write plays like his? Not unless we had the talent to go along with the tools. Similarly, all the bells and whistles and professional development in the world won't make a teacher a good teacher if the talent isn't there. Some people are good singers, dancers, or teachers while others aren't.

For far too long, those who hire teachers seem to think it's as easy as telling these new hires what to teach. Worse yet, teachers are often evaluated by folks who aren't good teachers themselves. How on earth would they be able to differentiate between good and bad teaching?

The first way Republicans can win on education is by starting at the top. Make sure that whoever is in charge of education at whatever agency—local, state, or federal—is a great teacher. Not simply a decent one but a spectacular one. Then, that person can hire only other spectacular teachers one by one to fill the administrative positions at primary and secondary schools. Those folks in turn would hire the teachers. That in itself would do wonders for American education, which at the moment is led by far too many bureaucrats who couldn't teach their way out of a paper bag.

Second, Republicans should create incentives for parents to attend school with their children, say, one night per week for two hours. Parents who want incentives such as tax cuts, tax credits, or public assistance must attend. Forty lessons over forty weeks—more than five absences total disqualifies the participants from any benefits.

Third, Republicans should promote the raising public school teachers' salaries dramatically but under three conditions.

1. No more unions. The profession will be exempt from union eligibility, but teachers already unionized will have the option to remain in the union or receive the salary increase.

2. Eliminate tenure.

3. Have the newly installed top-to-bottom great teachers determine the standards by which teachers will be evaluated, and make their job security subject to that criteria.

Let us turn back to the students who were pushed through the primary and secondary public school system without having acquired the skills to succeed in college. The solution is as simple as it sounds: stop that practice immediately. There should be no such concept as graduating on time or getting left back. Every person learns according to his or her abilities, motivation, effort, and other factors. Accordingly, students who haven't mastered a certain level of knowledge shouldn't proceed to the next level—period. Most important, there should be no stigma attached to that. It's better to graduate high school at age twenty having learned what was required than to graduate at age eighteen and having to use your fingers to determine what six and four equals.

Republicans can win on these issues by taking control of them and by hiring some of those great teachers as consultants. It's not enough for Republicans to bicker about teachers' unions—they must offer a better solution. Part of the solution means not to be like Democrats, particularly those same guilty white liberals who are so obsessed about not being perceived as racists that they'll push a child of color through to the next grade even if he or she isn't ready to advance. Without realizing it, they're doing that student a tremendous disservice.

Why not make school more fun? Why not have smaller classes and with children of all ages just like life at home? Why not encourage more learning communities, among, say, twenty families in neighborhoods all of whom meet regularly and evaluate the students in a well-monitored cohort?

These and other countless solutions are what Republicans need to adapt. But before they can come up with a better solution, they must understand the problem. Only then can they succeed in winning on education.

Tip 19: Winning on Guns

The right to bear arms and determining whether that right should be limited remains a hotly debated, politically divisive topic in America today. Both major parties fail to understand the issue adequately; even as they oppose one another, they're both wrong. Republicans were closer to being right until recently. Lately, they have veered out in the fringe, far from the vast American mainstream on this issue.

To understand the right to bear arms in the United States, we must take into consideration three concepts.

1. The Founding Fathers intended for individuals to have the right to bear arms.

2. That right is not what the Second Amendment is all about.

3. Just because the right to bear arms exists doesn't mean it's unlimited.

Then we can explore life today compared to when the Constitution was written and determine why some folks want to change with the times while others want to keep things as they were back then. The Constitution's Second Amendment reads, "A well regulated Militia, necessary to the security of a free State, the right of the people to keep and bear arms, shall not be infringed." Many Republicans think that amendment grants individuals the right to bear arms, but many Democrats think it grants only the right to establish a militia but doesn't give individuals that right. Both sides are somewhat wrong. Here's why.

Suppose the Founding Fathers wanted to guarantee that each state government would provide a basic education for all its people. Suppose that a new amendment—let's call it the Twenty-Eighth Amendment—used the format of the Second Amendment but changed the topic from guns to education: "A well regulated school system, necessary to the education of a free state, the right of the people to learn shall not be infringed." Clearly, such an amendment would not be about granting people the right to learn as that right is so obvious! The right guaranteed by the Twenty-Eighth Amendment would be a state-sponsored school system. There was no need for the Founding Fathers to expressly grant a right to bear arms because that right in 1787 was obvious. Instead, the Second Amendment guaranteed the right to a militia. We shall review why in a moment.

If you walk along a busy street in various neighborhoods in America and ask people, "Do you own a gun?" the answers are likely to be mixed. But if you ask those same folks, "Do you own a toothbrush?" is there anyone who'd say no? Owning a gun in 1787 was as common as is owning a toothbrush today. That's why that right was so obvious—like the right to eat and to breathe—that no one would even think it was necessary to place it in a constitutional amendment.

The real reason for the Second Amendment was to guarantee an armed force at the state level separate from the US military so that if the latter decided to overthrow the government and declare martial law, the state militia could issue a call to arms and protect its people. Remember, the Founders had gained independence from the tyrannical George III of England, and they were highly suspicious of creating a nation whose federal government would be all-powerful.

Most of us in the twenty-first century don't lose any sleep fearing that our nation's troops will storm Washington, throw the president, vice president, and members of Congress in jail, and take over. But quite amazingly, more than a few Americans live with that fear every day! They're paranoid about the government, and they believe that if the US armed forces decide to wage war on the people, they (and a handful of their buddies) have amassed enough firepower to fend them off!

Of course, most of us imagining a few well-armed renegades entrenched in a compound and fighting the US Army, Navy, Air Force, and Marines find the concept laughable, but those folks believe they could hold their own! That's why they don't want to part ways with their precious semiautomatics.

Turning now to the concept of limited rights, many folks don't realize that all our constitutional rights—every one of them—are limited. I cannot exercise my freedom of speech by threatening to kill someone. My neighbor cannot rob a bank every Friday night and claim it's part of his religion. You cannot distribute a leaflet that urges readers to commit a crime. And if the right to bear arms were absolute, the police would have no right to take guns away from the criminals they arrest. Yes, our jails would be filled with armed convicts if the right to bear arms were absolute.

Consider the two main types of people we have in the United States: loners and socializers. There are many more socializers than loners, but the loners aren't extinct. Socializers prefer to be part of society, to live in groups as ants, bees, wolves, and most other animal species do. They recognize they have to sacrifice some freedom such as the thrill of channeling their inner Rambos and shooting weapons built for war for the sake of the greater good of society. They see the United States as an extension of that society, an improved version of its European ancestor, England.

Loners, however, are like bears. They prefer to live alone. Sometimes miles and miles away from anyone else. They don't want to pay taxes. They don't want to receive services. They fend for themselves, and they don't see why everyone else shouldn't as well. They don't want a police force or care about one—they're quite happy defending themselves with their guns. They see the United States as the last bastion of freedom on earth, a country in which, as long as they don't intentionally set out to harm anyone, no one—not the police, the military, the governor, not even the president—can tell them what to do about anything. As those loners exist, the gun lobby will appeal to them, and the elected officials won't have the courage to stand up and do anything about it.

Republicans, on the one hand, should not cater to the gun lobby's whims. On the other hand, they should ensure law-abiding citizens that they support the individual right to bear arms, and that gun laws will be sensible so every law-abiding citizen who wants a gun and is fit to own one can do so.

But guns, like cars, should be registered, tracked, sold to, and used only by people who have been professionally trained to use them. And they should be of sound mind. That is the type of limitation that goes with the right.

Republicans should not be Democrats. They shouldn't insist that guns be limited to the military, to the police, and to each state's militia. But the types of weapons used and the ease with which they can be purchased is alarming, and the vast majority of the country is not afraid of regulating the process fairly but firmly. If the Republicans take that position, which is squarely aligned with that of the majority of Americans, they will win on the issue of guns.

Tip 20: Winning on Morality

Morality is generally defined as a system of values about what is good, right, and just. Some principles of morality are clearly defined in the United States, meaning that of 1,000 people surveyed, all 1,000, or at least 999, would agree that murder, rape, and robbing banks are immoral acts. Other issues are not as settled; a few hundred, perhaps as many as half of a group of 1,000, disagree about abortion, atheism, divorce, homosexuality, interracial marriage, premarital sex, and the use of alcohol, narcotics, and tobacco. These are heavily debated moral issues.

For the past few decades, the Republicans have staunchly defended their positions about unsettled notions of morality while violating clearly defined ones. They have been consistently pro-life in the case of abortion and have unequivocally stated that marriage ought to be a union between only a man and a woman. Though Republicans have been relentlessly uncompromising about these hotly debated issues, elected GOP officials have committed adultery, embezzlement, and other actions that violate clear moral standards.

"But Democrats commit adultery too," a defensive response might be. Ah, maybe so, but it looks worse when a Republican does it because of perception. Just as modern-day Democrats are reputed to be more racially sensitive than Republicans are, Republicans have long been the party of morality. If a Republican politician is heard behind closed doors uttering racial slurs, for example, that's damaging—but if a Democrat does it, that's more damaging because the Democrats are supposedly the champions in the fight against bigotry. By that measure, if a Democratic congressman cheats on his wife, that can be politically destructive, but if a Republican does so, that can be even more destructive considering Republicans are supposed to be the straight-laced, churchgoing, Boy and Girl Scouts on Capitol Hill.

Closely related to morality is transparency in government. Candidate Obama promised more government transparency—political discussions aired on C-SPAN and the like. But once he got into office, we saw very few examples of that, and the Republicans were right to chastise him for it. Unfortunately, their motives were based far less on principle than on catching him in a broken promise because their own subsequent presidential nominee, Mitt Romney, said next to nothing in 2012 about the need for more transparency in government. Neither did most of the Republican nominees, in fact, with one notable exception. Through twenty or so Republican primary debates, just about all Republican presidential candidates—at least all those who because of their backgrounds had a reasonable chance of establishing a following—participated in at least one of them, all except former Louisiana Governor and Congressman Buddy Roemer.

Roemer had been a Democrat who became a Republican. He was a private-sector businessman who ran a bank successfully without having taken a penny of federal bailout money. A sensible centrist, Roemer could have gained broad national appeal if he had had a better-organized and -staffed campaign team; he could have attracted disgruntled voters from both major parties as well as independents. At the very least, however, Roemer should have been given the chance to participate in the primary debates.

Consider that Herman Cain, a business executive and syndicated columnist who had never held political office and was hardly well known nationally at the time, was given a chance to take part in the debates. As a result, America got to witness on television Cain's warm personality, homespun wisdom, common business sense, and bold initiatives such as his 9–9–9 tax plan (a 9 percent tax on income, sales, and corporations as discussed in Tip 14: Winning on Taxes). Cain didn't win the nomination, but he soared in popularity and even enjoyed front-runner status for a short while. Eventually, he fell from grace because of allegations of an extramarital affair, but the debates had given him a chance to get his message across.

Why then were Cain and every other Republican candidate except Roemer allowed to debate? The GOP claimed it was because Roemer didn't meet specific eligibility thresholds involving poll rankings or funds raised, though Roemer put forth a plausible counterargument. He said—and many agree with him—that it was because he was the only candidate talking about eliminating special interests from politics. He advocated removing Political Action Committees (PACs) and Super PACs (i.e., big money) and ending secret backroom deals made by lobbyists. Roemer was also, in great part, the most outspoken critic of his fellow Republicans. Sure, he blasted President Obama and the Democrats as a whole on numerous issues, but so did every other Republican.

Where Roemer differed, however, was in that he didn't mince words when it came to pointing out the errors of his party's ways. Is it possible that the Republicans tried everything they could through their self-created debate-regulation loopholes to keep Roemer from opening his mouth on national television? We cannot be sure of the answer, but to win on transparency, the Republicans should never again deny a candidate of such stature a podium on the debate stage. As a former congressman and governor, Roemer was the only candidate in either major party who had executive and legislative experience (other than Obama himself, whose executive experience was his presidency; in 2008, he had none).

If the Republicans muster the intestinal fortitude to win on transparency and bring political discussions and negotiations far more into the public eye and to forego favorable treatment of big donors and their lobbyists, they will win the next election in a landslide.

They must win on morality. No politician should ever lie, steal, cheat, or commit any other illegal or immoral act. But Republicans in particular can reestablish their credibility by leading the way. Then, even if some folks disagree with them ideologically, they can still respect them for having values and not being hypocrites. That way, the Republicans can win on morality.

Conclusion

On November 6, 2012, rightwing pundits and voters were befuddled; how on earth had Obama won reelection? Everyone they knew had voted for Romney. And that spoke volumes. It was time they expanded their social and professional circles. But on November 4, 2014, this same group was in a much better mood because its beloved GOP had recaptured the Senate and maintained its stronghold on the House. And in 2016, they confidently dreamed the White House would be theirs too.

Although the political outcome of those two elections couldn't have been more different, the political IQ of these folks remained the same; they were clueless about why they had lost in 2012 and clueless about why they had won in 2014. They were like the kid in school who guesses on a multiple-choice exam and looks only at the final grade, not at the detailed explanation of each question and answer the professor provides as a learning tool. Hopefully, the Republican powers-that-be will turn to this book as their learning tool for how to win in 2016.

In that "bold colors, no pale pastels" speech Reagan delivered in 1975, he asked rhetorically, do we really need a third party? A third party potentially could reclaim the majority of America that's twisting in the wind at the moment, unwilling to stay with the Democrats or today's

Republicans for any meaningful length of time. The problem with third parties, however, is that as much as Americans fancy themselves outside-the-box innovators, they are really creatures of habit afraid to broaden their horizons, at least politically.

For years now, Congress's approval rating has been abysmal. More than 80 percent of the voters—year in, year out, regardless of which party is in charge—disapprove of the job Congress is doing. Unequivocally, that means the overwhelming majority of Americans are disgusted with Democrats and Republicans alike. Yet they continue to vote by a margin close to 99 percent for one of those two options. With rare exception, third-party politics in America is an afterthought.

Accordingly, though a third party might emerge—as the Republicans themselves did in 1860 and replaced the Whigs as the major-party alternative to the Democrats—it's far easier for one of the major parties to change from within and recapture its former glory.

This book's twenty tips have demonstrated exactly how that could be done. The Grumpy Old Party can become the Grand Old Party once again if its leaders and candidates learn to be more likable, pleasant, credible, bold, and intellectual. They must not be like Democrats, must not patronize and pander to Latinos, must not be flunkies for the conservative media, and must not resist compromise. They can reclaim populism, patriotism, race relations, and national security, and they can win on taxes, energy independence, immigration, religion, education, guns, and morality.

That's right, Republicans. You can no longer shrug your shoulders and claim you don't know why you continue to lose or come up with the same wrong reasons. In this book, you have been told how to win. The rest is up to you.

Afterword

In October 2014, while driving from the Rapid City Regional Airport in South Dakota to the nearby Custer State Game Lodge, where presidents Calvin Coolidge and Dwight D. Eisenhower stayed (each one's room now bearing his name), imagine my surprise as I noticed in a seemingly endless grassy field along the highway enormous statues of three presidents. Ronald Reagan (left) and George W. Bush. The statue not shown in the picture is that of John F. Kennedy. (I had to stop and take a closer look. My wife took the photo.) Rapid City is called the City of Presidents, as there are smaller statues of each one throughout its downtown district; it is also very close to Mount Rushmore.

It is fitting to close this book with an image of these two presidents because in the past fifty years, they conducted themselves more in line with the tips outlined in this book than did any other successful or unsuccessful GOP presidential nominee. Not so coincidentally, they are also the only two Republican presidents over the past fifty years to win and complete two full terms in office.

Epilogue: Remembering Jack Kemp

Jack Kemp is high on the list of great Americans who never became president. The NFL quarterback-turned-congressman who later became secretary of Housing and Urban Development (HUD) under the first President Bush, exemplified what the next Republican presidential nominee ought to be: smart, likable, well spoken, committed to well-conceptualized ideas, and able to work with the other side.

With no disrespect to George H. W. Bush or Bob Dole—the GOP nominees immediately following Ronald Reagan, two distinguished Americans who served their country honorably on the battlefield and in government—had America experienced eight years of President Kemp following eight years of President Reagan, the Republican Party would have cemented its place unequivocally as America's premier political party. The Democrats and other offshoots would have vied for a very small piece of the electoral pie.

Kemp was one of the most brilliant political thinkers of our time. His energy, innovativeness, and optimism knew no bounds. He would have been one of the great presidents.

Amid the limitless number of post-Reagan Republicans who have invoked his name, none was as much Reagan's true political heir as was Kemp. That the electorate failed to generate the type of adulation for

Kemp with which they showered Reagan is one of the greatest mysteries in contemporary American politics.

Kemp was the father of Reagan's famous tax cuts, which catapulted the economy out of its doldrums in the early 1980s and set it on a path of vigorous, inflation-free growth for nearly a generation. Like Reagan, he had boundless vision, unyielding hope, and limitless faith in the American people.

I have every reason to believe that had Kemp been elected president, he would have continued and even enhanced Reagan's policies. Rather than being a carbon copy of Reagan, Kemp was the ideal complement to Reagan and his mission. Whereas Reagan understood President Kennedy's philosophy that a rising tide lifts all boats, Kemp would have ensured that the boats were lifted more proportionately.

Kemp would have furthered the Reagan revolution. His passion for economic growth surpassed that of Reagan himself, and Kemp was even more of a populist. A self-proclaimed bleeding-heart conservative, Kemp created enterprise zones in troubled urban neighborhoods while HUD secretary, elevating them to unexpectedly high levels of prosperity. Kemp would have been the ideal person to channel the tremendous growth that Reagan orchestrated into opportunity for even more Americans than has been the case.

Jack Kemp passed away on May 2, 2009, which was the night of my bachelor party. Eerily, amid drinks, steaks, and cigars, a discussion arose about the future of the Republican Party, and a good friend of mine uttered something along the lines of, "Whatever happened to Jack Kemp?" Within the hour, we learned the sad news that Kemp had died. We toasted in his honor.

Kemp ran for the White House in 1988 but dropped out early on when he realized his campaign hadn't gained enough traction. I wrote to him a few months earlier, one of our few exchanges of correspondence, offering to help him win the White House. Here is an excerpt from his July 8, 1987 reply.

Dear Dino:

Your offer to help is heartening as I begin my campaign. We must stand together for our shared beliefs—promoting economic growth and opportunity, providing for a strong America and the growth of democratic values in all parts of the world, and enabling traditional family values to take root once again.

Index- Concordance

This index does not contain some references that appear on nearly every page (such as Republicans and United States) and general issues (such as abortion and immigration).

About the Author

Constantinos E. Scaros is a presidential historian specializing in voter behavior. He has taught history, political science, law, criminal justice, and journalism for over twenty years at numerous colleges and universities and is the author of several books: Learning about the Law, Learning about Immigration Law, All about Torts, Welcome to College, and Understanding the Constitution.

He is an attorney, newspaper editor, and political analyst as well. A lifelong Christian, he also writes extensively on matters of religion and spirituality.

Most importantly, he has been following politics closely since 1976 and has predicted every presidential election (ten and counting) correctly, several months in advance.

A native New Yorker, he lives with his family in Central Pennsylvania.

CPSIA information can be obtained at www.ICGtesting.com
Printed in the USA
LVOW08s1115140716

496317LV00001B/40/P

9 781512 713251